Assessment of Oak Woodland Resources in BLM's Eugene District

Lane County, Oregon

Technical Note 406

By:

David G. Chiller
Research Biologist, Pacific Wildlife Research Inc.

David G. Vesely
Senior Forest Ecologist, Pacific Wildlife Research Inc.

William I. Dean
Wildlife Biologist, Bureau of Land Management, Eugene District

Eugene District Office
2890 Chad Drive
Eugene, OR 97440-2226

June 2000

BLM/OR/WA/PL-00/052+6635

ABSTRACT

Because of the significant loss of oak (*Quercus* spp.) habitat and the subsequent increased value placed on oak woodlands for wildlife habitat, the preservation and restoration of native oak woodlands has become a priority for land managers and conservationists in the Western United States. In 1998, reconnaissance surveys were conducted on 13 oak woodland sites managed by the Bureau of Land Management's (BLM's) Eugene District in Lane County, Oregon. The sites were classified as either meadow-type communities or woodland-type communities; oak patches within the sites were delineated; and the topographic features, vegetation structure, and composition of the sites were characterized. Current conditions were then compared with conditions documented in historical records. In addition, the wildlife species most likely occurring on the sites were identified. Literature from oak woodland studies was then reviewed to determine whether certain management and restoration methods, such as eliminating conifer encroachment and thinning closed-canopy stands, would be effective in addressing conditions observed at the BLM sites.

ACKNOWLEDGMENTS

This work was part of a cooperative study, which involved the Oregon Department of Fish and Wildlife, The Nature Conservancy, Oregon and Washington Natural Heritage Program, and the Bureau of Land Management (BLM), to investigate oak woodland habitats. We would like to thank John Chatt, Carole Jorgensen, Lynn Larson, Cheshire Mayrsohn, and Chris Melotti for providing significant logistical support and encouragement throughout the development and implementation of this project. We would also like to thank Rebecca Goggans, Douglas Gomez, Joan Hagar, David Hibbs, Matt Hunter, Paula Larson, and Mike Reichenbach for their valuable contributions to an earlier draft of this report. Finally, we thank Eric Campbell and BLM's Oregon State Office for supporting the publication and distribution of this assessment, making it more available to other resource managers.

TABLE OF CONTENTS

FIGURES AND TABLES

Figures

Tables

INTRODUCTION

Oak Woodlands: Past and Present

The preservation and restoration of native oak (*Quercus* spp.) woodlands has recently become an important priority for land managers and conservationists in the western United States. This effort has been driven by a growing recognition of the significant loss of oak habitat and the subsequent "increased value placed on oak woodlands within the past 20 years, for esthetics, wildlife habitat, watershed functioning, outdoor recreation" and other qualities (Pillsbury et al. 1997).

In western Oregon, oak woodlands in the lowlands and neighboring foothills of the Willamette Valley have been heavily influenced by human activity for centuries (Johannessen et al. 1971). Extensive annual fires set by Native Americans prior to immigration of settlers in the 1840's, maintained open oak savannas and prairies and excluded tree species not adapted to frequent fire regimes (Cole 1977; Franklin and Dyrness 1988). Euro-Americans practiced fire suppression in the Willamette Valley, which has subsequently promoted development of closed-canopy woodlands composed of Oregon white oak (*Quercus garryana*), Douglas-fir (*Pseudotsuga menziesii*), big-leaf maple (*Acer macrophyllum*), and other tree species (Thilenius 1968). Agricultural land practices, tree harvesting, and urban development also have led to widespread changes in Willamette Valley landscapes (Towle 1982). In addition, the establishment of introduced plant species within oak woodlands and grasslands (Habeck 1961) has greatly altered plant community composition.

Despite these changes, existing oak environments continue to represent important and unique habitat for numerous wildlife species. In California, over 300 vertebrate species use oak-dominated woodlands for various purposes (Block et al. 1990). Oak woodlands in the Willamette Valley have a greater avian species diversity than Douglas-fir and western hemlock (*Tsuga heterophylla*) habitats (Anderson 1972) and provide a higher density of cavity resources (Gumtow-Farrior 1991). Not only do oaks provide resources for numerous species of wildlife that are known to use acorns (Christisen and Korschgen 1955), but the leaves and twigs of oak trees and associated plants provide resources for an undetermined number of additional vertebrate and invertebrate species (Verner 1980; Pavlik et al. 1991; Keator 1998). Conservation, effective management, and recognition of the value of oak woodlands will therefore be important to maintaining this region's wildlife diversity.

Oregon white oak, the most common oak species in the Willamette Valley and surrounding foothills, is most competitive at xeric or "poor" sites, which are areas that are dry and well-drained and areas that are droughty during the summer and poorly drained during the wet season (Stein 1990). In the absence of fire, Oregon white oaks are normally outcompeted at mesic sites not subjected to intense drought in summer (Thilenius 1964, 1968; Stein 1990). Therefore, Oregon white oak is often confined to borders or edges between two communities (McCulloch 1940), such as dry meadows and mature forests.

Assessment Objectives

In 1998, existing oak woodlands in the Bureau of Land Management's (BLM's) Eugene District in Oregon were identified and an assessment was conducted at selected sites. The objectives of the assessment were to:

❖ Describe the general physical and vegetation characteristics and conditions of each oak woodland and delineate woodland boundaries on aerial photos.

❖ Compare the current condition of selected sites with historical records using Oregon Natural Heritage Program vegetation classifications interpreted from General Land Office surveys conducted during the 1850's.

❖ Identify wildlife species most likely associated with the oak woodlands in the region surveyed based on distributions and habitat requirements of oak associated species and assess general suitability of available oak habitat for potentially occurring species.

❖ Review literature from studies relating to oak woodland management and restoration studies relevant to conditions observed at the study sites.

This assessment was in support of the district's efforts to preserve and effectively manage oak woodland habitats for associated wildlife species (USDI 1995).

Project Area

The oak woodlands surveyed lie within the McKenzie and South Valley Resource Areas (RA's) administered by BLM's Eugene District in Lane County, Oregon (Figure 1). Sites within the McKenzie RA occur on the approximate boundary of the Willamette Valley and Western Cascade physiographic provinces (Franklin and Dyrness 1988); those in the South Valley RA occur on the approximate boundary of the Willamette Valley and Coast Range provinces. These foothills are characterized by gentle slopes and valleys. Elevation of these sites was ≤2000 feet.

The climate of the Willamette Valley and surrounding foothills is temperate, with cool, wet winters and hot, dry summers. In Eugene, mean temperatures are 41 °F in January (min. 35 °F) and 67 °F in July (max. 81 °F); the average annual temperature is 53 °F. Annual precipitation averages 49.5 inches in Eugene, with more than 70 percent of rainfall occurring from November through March (Oregon Climate Service 1998).

The project area consists of a mosaic of vegetation characteristic of the pine-oak-fir (*Pinus-Quercus-Pseudotsuga*) vegetation zone

(Franklin and Dyrness 1988). This mosaic is composed of coniferous forests, oak woodlands, meadows, and forested wetland and riparian areas. Coniferous forests are dominated mainly by Douglas-fir with grand fir (*Abies grandis*), incense-cedar (*Calocedrus decurrens*), ponderosa pine (*Pinus ponderosa*), western redcedar (*Thuja plicata*) and western hemlock as associates. Big-leaf maple and Oregon white oak are common hardwood associates. Dominant understory species include dwarf Oregon grape (*Berbis nervosa*), California hazel (*Corylus cornuta* var. *californica*), salal (*Gaultheria shallon*), oceanspray (*Holodiscus discolor*), and sword fern (*Polystichum munitum*). Scattered grassy meadows on drier, south-facing slopes often contain Oregon white oak and pacific

madrone (*Arbutus menziesii*), with poison oak (*Rhus diversiloba*), oceanspray, and hazel as the most common shrubs. Wetland and riparian areas are commonly dominated by big-leaf maple in addition to Oregon ash (*Fraxinus latifolia*), which often extends into less moist areas. California black oak (*Q. kelloggi*) is limited to the southern parts of the surveyed area (Franklin and Dyrness 1988; and personal observations).

Private and public lands are highly interspersed on the McKenzie and South Valley RA's. Forestry and grazing have dominated land use on both public and private lands in the foothills. The floodplain of the Willamette River is the most densely populated region in Oregon.

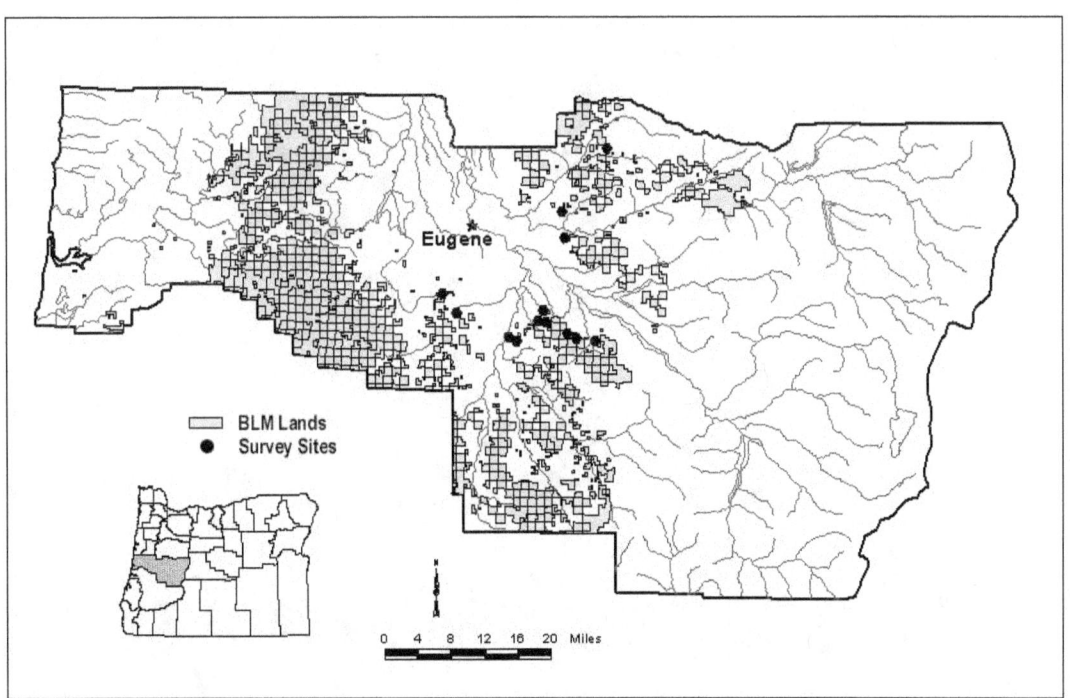

Figure 1. Map of Lane County, Oregon, showing the distribution and location of the 13 survey sites.

ASSESSMENT OF OAK WOODLAND RESOURCES IN BLM'S EUGENE DISTRICT

METHODS

Site Selection

Clusters of oak trees in the McKenzie and South Valley RA's were initially identified from field records and intra-agency communications. These locations were verified using aerial photos and field reconnaissance. The sites to be surveyed were then prioritized based on size and potential for timber and habitat management. One of the selected sites was actively managed for oak restoration prior to this survey. Selected sites were located within BLM parcels of forested land ranging from approximately 10-100 acres in size.

Site Classification

The sites were classified into two general types of oak communities:

❖ Meadow-type: Most oaks distributed along the perimeter of a small meadow having shallow soils, often on south-southwest aspects. Relatively larger oaks (height = 30-60 feet) occurred along the meadow perimeter with smaller individuals (often with shrubby form, 15-20 feet in height) scattered in central regions of meadows and were usually the only tree species growing in this central area. Meadows and associated oaks were generally elliptical in shape, surrounded by a Douglas-fir-dominated conifer matrix.

❖ Woodland-type: Woodlands were characterized by a uniform cohort of oaks (height = 60-80 feet) that were usually in dominant canopy positions or codominant with Douglas-fir or Oregon ash. Woodland sites typically bordered or were embedded within Douglas-fir-dominated conifer forests or wetland areas consisting of Oregon ash and big-leaf maple.

Oak Patch Delineation

Between August 12 and September 24, 1998, 13 sites were visited to delineate oak patches. At most sites, oak trees were distributed along a gradient of species composition: high concentrations of oaks arranged in small clusters or forming a ring around a meadow and gradually becoming less common in a forest matrix, usually dominated by Douglas-fir. Patch boundaries were based on five factors that were evaluated by the surveyor at each site:

1. Minimum patch area ≥1 acre.

2. Canopy composition: tree canopies at each patch were usually composed of more than 50 percent oak crowns.

3. Land ownership: non-BLM lands were excluded.

4. Topography: some boundaries were defined by sharp changes in slope or ridge lines.

5. "Compactness": boundaries were adjusted to facilitate management within oak patches and surrounding forest.

Site Descriptions

The topographic features, vegetation structure, and composition were characterized in 25 oak patches, which are listed in Table 1.

Table 1. List of surveyed sites, patch acronyms, and associated community types.

Site	Patch Acronym	Community Type
Anthony Creek	ANTH-1 ANTH-2 ANTH-3	Meadow
Bates	BATES	Meadow
Cougar Mountain	COUG-1 COUG-2	Woodland
Eagle's Rest	EAGL-1 EAGL-2	Woodland
Fox Hollow	FOX	Woodland
Gilkey Creek	GILK-1 GILK-2 GILK-3	Meadow
Kloster Mountain	KLOS-1 KLOS-2 KLOS-3 KLOS-4	Meadow
Rattlesnake	RATT-1 RATT-2 RATT-3	Meadow
Sears Road	SEARS	Woodland
Seventy-Ninth	SEVENT	Meadow
Weiss Road	WEISS	Meadow
Wendling	WEND-1 WEND-2	Meadow
Wills Road	WILLS	Woodland

Topography

Patch-level metrics (e.g., patch area, aspect, slope, elevation) and the location of patch centers including the respective units, methods, and instruments used, are shown in Table 2.

Patch Composition

Canopy

A modified form of guidelines from Cadwell (1998) was used to classify the vertical strata of tree canopies. Tree cover for each patch was divided into a maximum of three layers with at least a one-third difference in height between successive layers. For each layer, the absolute percent canopy cover for the patch, average top height of the layer, and total number of trees per acre were determined (Table 3). For the bottom canopy layer, trees <10 feet in height were not counted. To characterize the composition of each layer, the percent cover of the five most dominant species cohorts (species in an individual size class) with a relative canopy layer cover >5 percent was recorded (Table 4). Additional species observed were noted.

Table 2. Physical descriptors of individual patches including units and methods/instruments used.

Variable	Unit	Method/Instrument
Area	Nearest whole acre	Rangefinder and hip-chain
Aspect (average)	Degrees	Compass
Slope (average)	Degrees	Clinometer
Elevation	Nearest 50-foot interval	Topographic map
Location	UTM-Lat/Long	GPS

Table 3. Variables and methods used to characterize canopy layers within patches (three layers maximum).

Variable	Unit	Method/Instrument
Canopy cover	Percent of patch cover	Ocular estimate, absolute for each layer
Height	Nearest 10 feet	Average top of layer, rangefinder and clinometer
Trees per acre	Nearest whole number	100 percent tree count

Table 4. Descriptive variables for tree composition of individual canopy layers.

Variable	Unit	Method/Instrument
Percent of layer	Percent (multiple of 5)	Relative abundance of top five species by diameter class (min. 5 percent)
Diameter at breast height (dbh)	Diameter classes (inches): 0-5, 5-10, 10-15, 15-20, 20-30, 30-50	Ocular estimate; dbh tape, tape stick

Snags

The following data were recorded for each snag (completely dead tree) >10 inches dbh within each patch:

1. Type: either oak or other species.

2. Diameter class: 10-20 inches or >20 inches.

3. Structural classifications: a. Hard – trees with most of their branches and bark present and little sign of decay; b. Soft – trees commonly with tops broken off, lacking branches and bark (except *Pseudotsuga menziesii* and *Abies grandis*), with extensively decayed sapwood and heartwood (Parks et al. 1997).

Shrubs and Nonnative Plants

The five most common woody shrubs were recorded, along with percent of patch cover (nearest 5 percent). The presence of certain nonnative plants common to these habitats was also noted.

Oak Growth and Regeneration

To understand factors affecting oak growth in each site, an additional set of descriptors and variables was collected:

1. The general relative soil characteristics—moisture level, depth, and the presence of rocky outcrops—were noted.

2. To assess environmental and competitive factors potentially affecting oak growth, as well as the quality and quantity of wildlife habitat, the general form of oaks according to the degree of openness/width of tree crowns and locations within the patch where form varied were noted.

3. The relative abundance of oak regeneration (oak trees with dbh <3 inches and height <10 feet) in each patch was noted using ocular estimation:

    a. Absent.

    b. Rare, ~1-20 stems per acre.

    c. Common, ~21-50 stems per acre.

    d. Abundant, >50 stems per acre.

4. In addition, increment core samples were obtained from one or two trees at each patch. Open-form trees were cored to study oak diameter growth rates in the absence of competition. When open-form trees were not present, cores were taken from relatively older trees with the widest crowns, and consequently, the least (relative) amount of competition from neighbors. Core samples were taken at breast height and were used to estimate growth rates or rings per inch (RPI) and age (either by counting growth rings or using RPI x tree radius at breast height if cores were not complete). Height, diameter at breast height, and mean crown radius were also measured for each cored tree. In addition, at two of the meadow-type communities, a single tree was harvested along with numerous shorter, shrubby clusters of oak stems. The complete cross section produced from these stems provided a more accurate estimate of age and growth rates in these thin, slow-growing stems.

Additional Descriptive Information

One or two photographs were taken (using a 35mm SLR camera with a 28mm lens) and maps were sketched of each patch to provide additional visual references of oak distribution. Evidence of grazing (e.g., presence of fencing) and tree harvesting, as well as off-road use, vandalism, and dumping, was recorded at each location. In some sites, searches were performed outside of the patch boundaries to determine the presence, distribution, and general condition of neighboring oak communities and to assist in the understanding of the vegetation history at that site.

Oak Distribution Patterns

A combination of survey information and the interpretation of historic land survey records was used to characterize the vegetation history and trends occurring at each site. During the 1850's, the U.S. General Land Office (GLO) conducted land surveys in the Willamette Valley to designate township and sections and determine lands suitable for settlement. Experienced surveyors used large "bearing" or "witness" trees to mark township and sectional boundaries in addition to making general vegetation and environmental descriptions (Habeck 1961). Christy et al. (1996) have used the transcriptions and plat maps of the GLO surveyors and soil maps to create classifications of historic vegetation types for the surveyed areas within Lane County. These classifications have been transcribed into databases, which can be used to produce geographic information system (GIS) maps of historical vegetation (see Christy et al. 1996 for detailed protocol).

Two vegetation classifications were available from these maps for characterizing historic vegetation at the oak sites: major vegetation types and subcategories of these major types. Subcategory information was not available for all sites and GLO survey information was completely lacking for two sites. The four major types of vegetation occurring at or near sites are listed below with definitions according to Christy et al. (1997):

❖ Closed forest upland: Distance to witness trees (large, marker trees used to establish boundaries of townships and sections) was

<66 feet, typically <33 feet. Stands may include fire-sensitive species such as cedar, hemlock, and maple.

❖ Woodland: Distance to witness trees mostly 66-132 feet. Stands usually lack cedar, hemlock, and maple.

❖ Savanna: Openings with grass, fern, hazel, and shrub oak understory. Distance to witness trees mostly >132 feet.

❖ Prairie: Distance to witness trees mostly 132-528 feet. Understory with grass or fern, with no reference to dense shrub growth.

Wildlife Habitat Associations

Wildlife Species

To identify species most likely occurring in the surveyed sites in Lane County, Oregon, a list of wildlife species associated with the observed habitats was compiled using information from Brown (1985) and Csuti et al. (1997). Three plant communities were selected from Brown (1985) that most closely represented those at the surveyed sites: dry-hillside/grass-forb, deciduous-hardwood; and conifer-hardwood. In order to focus on species most strongly associated with the selected community types, only species breeding in these habitats were listed. The use of edge habitats and specific information on required habitat structural components (snags and cavities) for the selected species were also noted. Because

Brown (1985) does not directly specify species associated with oaks, habitat information from Csuti et al. (1997) was included to help identify which of the selected species are known to use oak woodlands. Some of the limited oak-habitat relationship information for the Willamette Valley was included by listing relative bird abundance information from Hagar and Stern (1997). From this list and other sources, ten species that are commonly associated with oaks were chosen and the use of oak habitat for five of these species was described.

Formal wildlife surveys were not conducted; however, any sign or direct observation of wildlife species was noted during vegetation surveys.

Habitat Components

Oak-related literature was reviewed to evaluate the relationships between animal populations and Oregon white oak plant communities. Acorn production in each patch was estimated

using relationships described by Goodrum et al. (1971). Using counts of trees per acre and the relative abundance of oak cohorts (dbh class) in each canopy layer, as well as additional field notes, the number of trees was estimated by size class at each surveyed patch. The mast production was then calculated for the size classes producing acorns according to the following approximated yields from Goodrum et al. (1971; table 2): 10-15 inches dbh = 5.48 pounds; 15-20 inches = 11.05 pounds; 20-25 inches = 16.65 pounds; 25-30 inches = 20.5 pounds.

Restoration and Management Literature Review

Oak woodland management and restoration literature that addressed the specific conditions observed at the surveyed sites was reviewed in order to aid future management decisions for these areas.

Overview of BLM Sites

Physiography

The BLM sites surveyed ranged from 750 to 2,000 feet above sea level (Table 5). The sites most often occurred on xeric, south and southwest hill slopes, although some sites (e.g., Eagle's Rest, Fox Hollow) occurred in lower topographic positions and had moist or wet soils.

Plant Community Composition and Structure

Dominant tree canopy positions in woodland-type patches and adjacent to meadow-type patches were most often occupied by Douglas-fir, with incense-cedar and Oregon white oak occasionally codominant (Table 6). Pacific madrone was often observed on xeric sites.

Oregon ash, grand fir, and big-leaf maple were also common.

Oregon white oak occurred in small patches (maximum area = 5 acres) at the 13 BLM sites, and oak crowns usually formed a minor component of the overall canopy (mean = 18 percent cover, max. = 54 percent cover) (Table 7). Oak trees >15 inches dbh were rare at the BLM sites and dry sites on south and southwest aspects were dominated by a cohort of shrubby oaks <5 inches dbh.

Snags were uncommon structural features in the surveyed BLM woodlands (Table 8). The greatest total density measured was 8.5 snags/acre (COUG-1) and snags >20 inches

Table 5. Summary of physical characteristics of surveyed patches (N= 25 for all variables).

	Elevation (feet)	Slope (°)	Aspect (°)	Acres
Mean	1,264.0	18.9	187.6	2.6
Max.	2,000.0	47.0	290.0	5.0
Min.	750.0	5.0	72.0	1.0

dbh were very rare (maximum observed density = 0.75/acre). Although the number or volume of dead branches in the surveyed sites was not measured, it was subjectively estimated that dead branches on live oak trees represented a considerable fraction of the small diameter (<10-inch diameter) cavity nesting substrate in these woodlands.

Poison oak was the most frequently observed shrub (88 percent of patches) at oak patches

(Table 9). Oceanspray and Himalayan blackberry (*Rubus discolor*) were also observed at more than half the patches surveyed.

Most sites were occupied by one or more plant species listed by the BLM as nonnative plants (Table 10); however, only Himalayan blackberry and Scotch broom were abundant within oak patches.

Table 6. Summary of the most abundant tree cohorts (based on species and size) occurring in canopy layers in each surveyed patch. Patches are listed according to community type: M= meadow, W= woodland. Cohort 1 and 2 (C1 and C2) represent the species of the two most dominant tree cohorts for each layer; a dashed line indicates that either only one species occurred in the top layer or the canopy consisted of only two layers (top and bottom). Multiple cohorts indicate equal dominance. ABGR= grand fir; ACMA= big leaf maple; ARME = Pacific madrone; CADE= incense-cedar; FRLA = Oregon ash; PSME = Douglas-fir; QUGA = Oregon white oak.

| Patch | Community Type | Canopy Layer | | | | | |
		Top C1	C2	Middle C1	C2	Bottom C1	C2
ANTH-1	M	PSME	CADE	QUGA	ARME	QUGA	QUGA
ANTH-2	M	ARME	ARME	-	-	QUGA	ARME
ANTH-3	M	PSME	-	ARME	ARME	QUGA	ARME/PSME
BATES	M	PSME	PSME	QUGA	ARME	QUGA	QUGA
GILK-1	M	PSME	PSME	QUGA	QUGA	QUGA	CADE
GILK-2	M	PSME	CADE	CADE	PSME	QUGA	PSME
GILK-3	M	PSME	PSME	QUGA	CADE/PSME	QUGA	PSME
KLOS-1	M	PSME	-	-	-	QUGA	ARME/PSME
KLOS-2	M	PSME	CADE	QUGA	ACMA/ARME/CADE	QUGA	QUGA
KLOS-3	M	PSME	-	QUGA	ACMA/ARME/CADE	QUGA	QUGA/PSME
KLOS-4	M	PSME	-	QUGA	ARME/QUGA	QUGA	ARME/PSME
RATT-1	M	PSME	PSME	QUGA	PSME	QUGA	PSME
RATT-2	M	PSME	PSME	QUGA	ACMA/PSME	QUGA	ACMA/PSME
RATT-3	M	PSME	PSME	QUGA	QUGA	QUGA	ACMA/PSME
SEVENT	M	PSME	-	QUGA	ARME/QUGA/PSME	QUGA	QUGA
WEISS	M	PSME	PSME	PSME	PSME	PSME	QUGA
WEND-1	M	QUGA	QUGA	-	-	QUGA	QUGA
WEND-2	M	PSME	-	QUGA	QUGA	QUGA	QUGA
COUG-1	W	PSME	ABGR/PSME	QUGA	ABGR	ABGR	QUGA
COUG-2	W	CADE	QUGA	-	-	ABGR	CADE
EAGL-1	W	QUGA	QUGA	-	-	FRLA	ABGR/PSME/QUGA
EAGL-2	W	QUGA	PSME	PSME	FRLA	FRLA	PSME
FOX	W	PSME	PSME	PSME	ACMA/FRLA/PSME	PSME	QUGA
SEARS	W	PSME	PSME	QUGA	QUGA	PSME	QUGA
WILLS	W	PSME	PSME	QUGA	QUGA	QUGA	QUGA

Table 7. Summary of selected oak size characteristics for each surveyed patch. Patches are listed according to community types: M= meadow, W= woodland. For each patch, the size class, percent cover for the entire patch, and the respective canopy layer height values are given for the oak cohort with the greatest patch cover and the largest size class (dbh).

Patch	Community Type	Area (acres)	Oak Cohort with Greatest Patch Cover			Oak Cohort with Largest Diameter Class		
			dbh Class (in)	Percent Cover	Layer Height (feet)	dbh Class (in)	Percent Cover	Layer Height (feet)
ANTH-1	M	1	0-5	14	20	10-15	1	40
ANTH-2	M	2	5-10	3	30	10-15	1	30
ANTH-3	M	2	5-10	4	30	5-10	4	30
BATES	M	3	0-5	15	25	5-10	12	40
GILK-1	M	2	10-15	12	50	10-15	12	50
GILK-2	M	1	5-10	3	30	15-20	2	70
GILK-3	M	2	10-15	8	60	10-15	8	60
KLOS-1	M	3	5-10	8	50	5-10	8	50
KLOS-2	M	3	0-5	18	20	5-10	2	40
KLOS-3	M	5	0-5	8	20	5-10	4	40
KLOS-4	M	3	0-5	21	20	10-15	1	40
RATT-1	M	4	5-10	8	40	10-15	2	40
RATT-2	M	3	10-15	8	30	10-15	4	50
RATT-3	M	4	5-10	8	20	10-15	4	40
SEVENT	M	2	0-5	54	15	5-10	14	40
WEISS	M	3	15-20	2	70	15-20	2	70
WEND-1	M	2	5-10	21	35	10-15	3	35
WEND-2	M	3	5-10	14	30	5-10	14	30
COUG-1	W	2	10-15	21	70	15-20	7	70
COUG-2	W	2	10-15	21	80	10-15	21	80
EAGL-1	W	1	10-15	45	80	10-15	45	80
EAGL-2	W	2	10-15	48	80	15-20	8	80
FOX	W	2	5-10	18	40	10-15	7	70
SEARS	W	5	10-15	28	80	15-20	3	80
WILLS	W	2	10-15	28	80	15-20	14	80

Table 8. List of snag counts and characteristics for each surveyed patch. Patches are listed according to community type: M = meadow and W = woodland. Size classes are dbh (inches). Refer to Methods section for definition of hard and soft characteristics.

| Patch | Community Type | Oaks | | | | Other Species | | | | Total |
| | | Hard | | Soft | | Hard | | Soft | | |
		10-20	>20	10-20	>20	10-20	>20	10-20	>20	
ANTH-1	M	0	0	0	0	0	0	0	0	0
ANTH-2	M	0	0	0	0	0	0	0	0	0
ANTH-3	M	0	0	0	0	0	0	0	0	0
BATES	M	0	0	0	0	0	0	3	4	7
COUG-1	W	0	0	0	0	3	1	11	2	17
COUG-2	W	1	0	1	0	7	0	1	0	10
EAGL-1	W	0	0	4	0	0	0	2	0	6
EAGL-2	W	2	0	3	0	0	0	0	0	5
FOX	W	0	0	1	0	1	2	1	3	8
GILK-1	M	0	0	0	0	0	1	0	0	1
GILK-2	M	0	0	0	0	0	0	0	0	0
GILK-3	M	0	0	0	0	2	5	0	0	7
KLOS-1	M	0	0	0	0	0	0	0	0	0
KLOS-2	M	0	0	0	0	0	0	0	0	0
KLOS-3	M	0	0	0	0	0	0	0	0	0
KLOS-4	M	0	0	0	0	0	0	0	0	0
RATT-1	M	0	1	0	0	0	0	0	4	5
RATT-2	M	1	0	0	0	0	0	0	0	1
RATT-3	M	0	0	0	0	2	0	2	0	4
SEARS	W	2	1	8	2	0	1	3	0	17
SEVENT	M	0	0	0	0	1	0	0	0	1
WEISS	M	0	0	1	0	2	2	1	0	6
WEND-1	M	0	0	0	0	0	0	0	0	0
WEND-2	M	0	0	0	0	0	1	0	0	1
WILLS	W	1	0	4	0	1	1	2	0	9
	Total	7.0	2.0	22.0	2.0	19.0	14.0	26.0	13.0	105.0
	Mean	0.3	0.1	0.9	0.1	0.8	0.6	1.0	0.5	4.2

Table 9. Percent occurrence of the most dominant shrubs in the surveyed patches. Numbers in parentheses = number of patches. Total number of patches surveyed = 25.

Shrub	Percent Occurrence
Poison oak	88 (22)
Oceanspray	60 (15)
Himalayan blackberry	56 (14)
California hazel	44 (11)
Orange honeysuckle	40 (10)
Tall Oregon grape	36 (9)
Trailing blackberry	36 (9)
Common snowberry	32 (8)

Table 10. Percent occurrence of nonnative plants observed in the surveyed patches. Numbers in parentheses = number of patches. Total number of patches surveyed = 25.

Nonnative Plant	Percent Occurrence
St. John's wort	64 (16)
Tansy ragwort	60 (15)
Himalayan blackberry	56 (14)
Bull thistle	40 (10)
Scotch broom	32 (8)
Evergreen blackberry	32 (8)
Canada thistle	8 (2)

Oak Growth and Regeneration

Diameter (dbh), height, diameter growth (RPI), and estimated ages were measured for 20 sample Oregon white oaks located on the BLM sites (Table 11). On average, diameter growth was 21.0 RPI (range = 7.8-45.8). Thilenius (1964) reported mean diameter growth (RPI) =12.5 among "forest-form" or closed canopy trees (12-21 inches dbh). Stein (1990) reported that 16-20 RPI is typical among Oregon white oaks. Relationships between sample tree attributes are represented in Figures 2A-D. Estimates of oak regeneration for each patch are shown in Table 12.

Table 11. Growth and age information for sampled oak trees. Patches are listed according to community type: M = meadow and W = woodland. dbh= diameter at breast height, RPI = rings per inch. The #1 and #2 following a patch name indicates two different cores taken at the same patch.

Patch	Community Type	dbh (inches)	Height (feet)	RPI	Estimated Age (years)	Mean Crown Radius (feet)
ANTH-3	M	8.5	32	22.2	59	9.5
BATES	M	11.0	30	21.3	88	8.3
GILK-2	M	17.0	64	13.0	111**	17.3
GILK-3	M	13.0	75	27.4	178**	10.0
KLOS-1	M	11.5	50	12.3	58	9.5
KLOS-3*	M	3.5	21	45.8	50	
KLOS-4	M	7.0	30	19.0	53	7.5
RATT-3	M	16.0	35	8.3	67**	14.0
SEVENT	M	14.0	42	26.7	187**	8.8
WEISS (#1)	M	11.5	28	7.8	39	12.5
WEISS (#2)	M	15.0	70	18.0	100	10.8
WEND-2 (#1)	M	7.5	30	22.1	50	5.0
WEND-2* (#2)	M	3.0	24	33.6	47	
COUG-1	W	19.5	62	25.7	251**	10.8
COUG-2	W	22.0	70	15.0	165**	9.3
EAGL-1	W	12.5	85	22.5	134	13.0
EAGL-2	W	15.5	80	16.7	130**	13.3
FOX	W	12.0	65	28.4	170**	8.8
SEARS	W	21.0	62	15.8	166**	12.8
WILLS	W	14.5	85	17.8	129**	9.
	Mean	12.8	52.0	21.0	68	10.6

* cuttings or very small stems for which canopy radii were not measured.
** age was estimated (rings per inch x radius at breast height).

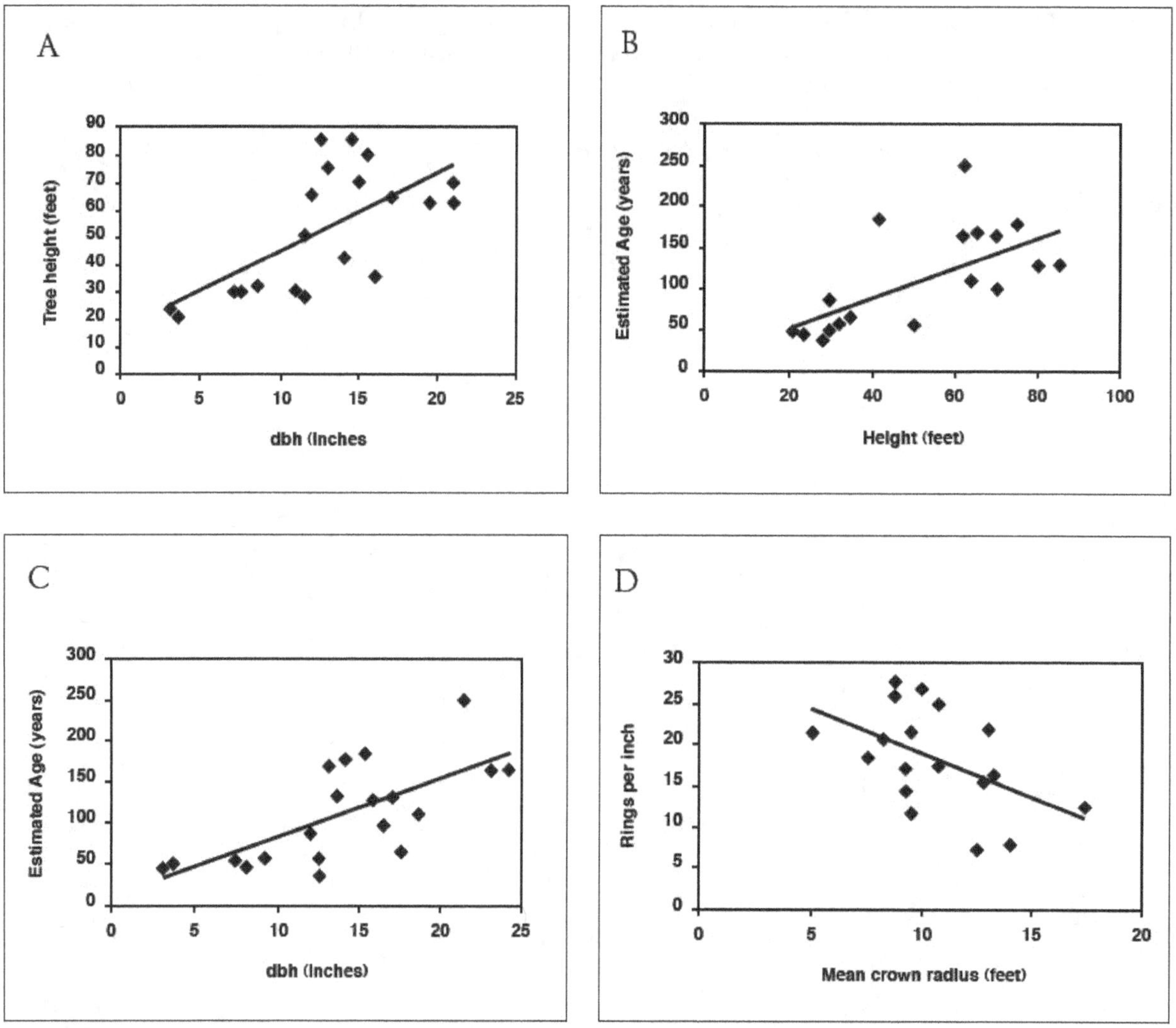

Figures 2A-D. Relationships between (A) tree height and dbh, (B) tree age and height, (C) tree age and dbh, and (D) growth rate (rings per inch) and mean crown radius for sampled oaks.

Table 12. Estimates of oak regeneration abundance (oak stems with dbh <3 inches and height <10 feet) in the surveyed patches. Patches are listed according to community type: M = meadow, W = woodland. Rare ~1-20 stems per acre; common ~21-50 stems per acre. Area estimated to nearest acre.

Patch	Oak Regeneration	Community Type	Area (acres)
ANTH-1	Rare	M	1
ANTH-2	Absent	M	2
ANTH-3	Absent	M	2
BATES	Common	M	3
GILK-1	Common	M	2
GILK-2	Common	M	1
GILK-3	Common	M	2
KLOS-1	Rare	M	3
KLOS-2	Common	M	3
KLOS-3	Common	M	5
KLOS-4	Common	M	3
RATT-1	Rare	M	4
RATT-2	Rare	M	3
RATT-3	Rare	M	4
SEVENT	Rare	M	2
WEISS	Rare	M	3
WEND-1	Rare	M	2
WEND-2	Common	M	3
COUG-1	Rare	W	2
COUG-2	Rare	W	2
EAGL-1	Rare	W	1
EAGL-2	Rare	W	2
FOX	Common	W	2
SEARS	Rare	W	5
WILLS	Common	W	2

Site Descriptions

Anthony Creek

Site: south aspect; soil appears shallow in meadow; xeric.

Oak distribution: three clusters of small (≤2-acre) meadow-type communities.

Vegetation structure: top canopy layers dominated by Douglas-fir, Pacific madrone, and incense-cedar; oak canopy cover ~14 percent; oaks >5 inches dbh are rare (≤5 percent cover).

Oak growth rate: sample tree height was 32 feet (dbh = 8.5 inches) at 59 years.

Regeneration: oak seedlings were very rare; some sprouts on fire-scarred trees were observed; conifer regeneration is rare.

Management issues: none noted.

1850's land cover: closed upland forest.

Bates

Site: hilltop position; steeper slopes than average; xeric to mesic conditions.

Oak distribution: single meadow-type community; approximately 3 acres; oaks interspersed with madrone and Douglas-fir.

Vegetation structure: top canopy layer dominated by Douglas-fir; oak canopy cover ~15 percent; largest oaks are in 10- to 15-inch dbh class; dense shrub layer; poison oak cover ≥90 percent.

Oak growth rate: sample tree height was 30 feet (dbh = 11.0 inches) at 88 years.

Regeneration: abundant vegetative sprouts from live trees.

Management issues: sensitive plant area.

1850's land cover: woodland.

Cougar Mountain

Site: south aspect; hillside position; moist soil (spring observed near Coug-2).

Oak distribution: two small (2-acre) woodland-type communities; oaks also occurred on adjacent private lands to the east at Coug-1.

Vegetation structure: top canopy layer dominated by Douglas-fir, incense-cedar, grand fir, and oak; oak canopy cover ~21 percent; largest oaks are in 25- to 30-inch dbh class; conifer succession apparent; Himalayan blackberry cover ≥20 percent.

Oak growth rate: sample tree #1 height was 62 feet (dbh = 19.5 inches) at ~250 years; sample tree #2 height was 70 feet (dbh = 22.0 inches) at ~165 years.

Regeneration: very rare oak reproduction observed; conifer regeneration is common.

Management issues: compacted soils from bike trail (Coug-1); old fencing (Coug-2).

1850's land cover: prairie; closed upland forest.

Eagle's Rest

Site: northwest aspect; lower slope position; seasonal wetlands observed.

Oak distribution: two small (≤2-acre) woodland-type communities; oaks continue to adjacent private lands.

Vegetation structure: top canopy layer is dominated by oak and Douglas-fir; oak canopy cover ~50 percent; largest oaks are in 20- to 25-inch dbh class; numerous dead branches on live trees; Himalayan blackberry cover ≥90 percent at Eagl-2.

Oak growth rate: sample tree #1 height was 85 feet (dbh = 12.5 inches) at 134 years; sample tree #2 height was 80 feet (dbh = 15.5 inches) at ~130 years.

Regeneration: oak reproduction is rare; Oregon ash and Douglas-fir regeneration is common.

Management issues: fencing on west property line at Eagl-2; blackberry density indicates possible grazing; minor amounts of garbage.

1850's land cover: described as "mountainous and unfit for habitation."

Fox Hollow

Site: lower slope-riparian position; moist soil.

Oak distribution: single, small (~2-acre) woodland-type community; a reconnaissance of neighboring areas revealed scattered oaks (height range 30-70 feet, 5-15 inches dbh), one massive individual (approximately 26 inches dbh)

is located approximately 200 feet south of the patch across a small stream.

Vegetation structure: top canopy layer dominated by Douglas-fir; oak canopy cover ~18 percent; largest oaks are in 15- to 20-inch dbh class; this was the only BLM site where California black oak was observed (*Quercus kelloggi*), representing approximately 20 percent of all oaks at this site; oaks in middle and bottom canopy position appeared to be of low vigor; conifer succession apparent; dense shrub layer.

Oak growth rate: sample tree height was 65 feet (dbh = 12.0 inches) at ~170 years.

Regeneration: oak seedlings common in canopy gaps; conifer regeneration is also common.

Management issues: insect infestation problem on oak foliage.

1850's land cover: woodlands and forests composed of Douglas-fir, chinquapin, and madrone on south slopes; Douglas-fir and bigleaf maple on north slopes; also incense-cedar, oak, grand fir, western redcedar, Pacific yew, red alder, and pacific dogwood.

Gilkey Creek

Site: south-facing slopes; dry soils in meadows.

Oak distribution: three small (≤2-acre) meadow-type communities; oaks continue to bordering private lands at each patch.

Vegetation structure: top-canopy dominated by Douglas-fir, oak canopy cover ~12 percent; largest oaks in15- to 20-inch dbh class; majority of oaks 10 to15 inches dbh; relatively tall (30- to 60-foot) oaks in meadow center at Gilk-1; all trees overtopped in Gilk-2.

Oak growth rate: sample tree #1 height was 64 feet (dbh = 17.0 inches) at ~111 years; sample tree #2 height was 75 feet (dbh = 13 inches) at ~178 years.

Regeneration: common, mainly vegetative sprouting; conifer regeneration is common.

Management issues: compacted off-road trails (Gilk-1 and -2).

1850's land cover: savanna and prairie bordering closed forest upland.

Kloster Mountain

Site: steep hillside meadows, with south aspect dry soils and numerous rocky outcrops.

Oak distribution: four meadow-type communities (≤5 acres); embedded in a conifer matrix.

Vegetation structure: upper canopy dominated by Douglas-fir and some incense cedar; oak canopy cover ~21 percent; largest oaks 10-15 inches dbh; oaks >10 inches dbh rare (<10 percent cover).

Oak growth rate: sample tree #1 height was 50 feet (dbh = 11.5 inches) at 58 years; sample #2 height was 21 feet (dbh = 3.5 inches) at 50 years; sample tree #3 height was 30 feet (dbh 7.0 inches) at 53 years.

Management issues: minor amount of logging operation debris.

Regeneration: common, mainly vegetative sprouting.

1850's land cover: unclassified.

Rattlesnake

Site: upslope meadows varying in aspect.

Oak distribution: three meadow-type communities (≤4 acres); reconnaissance south of Ratt-2 revealed three small oak clusters in openings of ~0.75 acres (height range 30-50 feet, with one individual >80 feet, ~25 inches dbh; two clusters were likely on private land).

Vegetation structure: upper canopy dominated by Douglas-fir; oak canopy cover ~8 percent; largest oaks 25-30 inches dbh, but rare (<1 percent cover); majority of oaks growing under conifers.

Oak growth rate: sample tree height was 35 feet (dbh = 16.0 inches) at ~67 years.

Management issues: sensitive plant site (Ratt-1).

Regeneration: oak and conifer regeneration are rare.

1850's land cover: woodland and closed forest upland.

Sears Road

Site: lower slope bordering forested uplands, riparian area, and open savanna.

Oak distribution: single woodland-type community (~5 acres) merging with open grassland/savanna.

Vegetation structure: upper canopy dominated by Douglas-fir; oak canopy cover ~28 percent; large open grown oaks (30-40 inches dbh; <1 percent cover) overtopped by conifers at woodland/savanna edge; Himalayan blackberry cover (≥90 percent cover) mainly under closed canopy woodland.

Oak growth rate: sample tree height was 62 feet (dbh = 21.0 inches) at ~166 years.

Management issues: fenceline on north-south property boundary.

Regeneration: oak regeneration is rare; conifer regeneration is common.

1850's land cover: prairie.

Seventy-Ninth

Site: hillside meadow with northwest aspect; well-drained soils; embedded in forested uplands.

Oak distribution: single long thin meadow-type community (could be classified as unique woodland-type with shrub-form oaks) (~2 acres); ~25 oaks (50-70 feet) observed in canopy gap 100 yards northeast of surveyed patch.

Vegetation structure: upper canopy dominated by Douglas-fir; oak canopy cover ~54 percent; majority of trees with thin shrubby stems; largest oaks are 10-15 inches dbh; dense shrub layer (oceanspray cover ~70 percent).

Oak growth rate: sample tree height was 42 feet (dbh =14.0 inches) at ~187 years.

Management issues: water line at extreme east end of patch (exact property line not defined).

Regeneration: oak regeneration is rare; conifer regeneration is common.

1850's land cover: closed forest upland.

Weiss Road

Site: lower slope meadow; bordering riparian area.

Oak distribution: single meadow-type community (~3 acres total); adjoining private land to north, which contains oaks with large relic oak snag.

Vegetation structure: upper canopy dominated by Douglas-fir; oak canopy cover ~2 percent, largest oaks are in 20- to 25-inch dbh class.

Oak growth rate: sample tree #1 height was 28 feet (dbh = 11.5 inches) at 39 years; sample tree #2 height was 70 feet (dbh = 15.0 inches) at 100 years.

Management issues: site adjacent to logging road; dumping along road near patch.

Regeneration: oak regeneration is rare; conifer regeneration is common.

1850's land cover: woodland.

Wendling

Site: lower slope position; dry soils.

Oak distribution: two meadow-type communities (≤3 acres).

Vegetation structure: upper canopy dominated by Douglas-fir and oak; oak canopy cover ~21 percent, largest oaks 15-20 inches dbh; management activities prior to surveys included conifer snag creation and removal of dense scotch broom cover.

Oak growth rate: sample tree #1 height was 30 feet (dbh = 7.5 inches) at 50 years; sample tree #2 height was 24 feet (dbh = 3.0 inches) at 47 years.

Management issues: patches adjacent to road.

Regeneration: oak regeneration is rare; conifer regeneration is common.

1850's land cover: woodlands and forests composed of Douglas-fir, chinquapin, and madrone on south slopes; Douglas-fir and big-leaf maple on north slopes; also incense-cedar, oak, grand fir, western redcedar, Pacific yew, red alder, and pacific dogwood.

Wills Road

Site: lower slope-riparian position; seasonally wet soil.

Oak distribution: small (≤2-acre) single open woodland-type community; scattered oaks (height = 20–70 feet) bordering conifer matrix in canopy openings.

Vegetation structure: upper canopy dominated by Douglas-fir; oak canopy cover ~28 percent; largest oaks 25-30 inches dbh.

Oak growth rate: sample tree #1 height was 85 feet (dbh = 14.5 inches) at ~129 years.

Management issues: evidence of oak harvesting near patch (1 stump 10-15 inches dbh).

Regeneration: oak regeneration is common; conifer regeneration is common.

1850's land cover: woodland and closed forest upland.

Oak Distribution Patterns

Regional Level

Most Oregon forests are dominated by conifers. Hardwoods often function as pioneer species or are confined to local niches (Franklin and Dyrness 1988). In western Oregon, oak woodlands are concentrated in the interior valleys (Franklin and Dyrness 1988) where larger, fire-resistant oaks were able to survive the frequent fires that eliminated younger trees, creating open savanna and prairies in many areas (Thilenius 1968). The increase in closed canopy conditions in oak woodlands resulting from active fire suppression often favors seedling growth of conifers such as Douglas-fir (Barnhart et al. 1987). Several authors (Sprague and Hansen 1946; Habeck 1961; Thilenius 1964; Franklin and Dyrness 1988) have discussed potential climax communities succeeding oaks under continued fire control. In general, they conclude that the climax community is most likely conifer forest dominated by grand fir and/or Douglas-fir; however, this will vary according to specific conditions and existing vegetation.

Patch Level

Meadow-Type Sites

The influence of environmental conditions and competition are demonstrated by examining the nature of oak and conifer growth and distribution typical of meadow-type sites. Figure 3 depicts the typical tree distribution occurring along hypothetical environmental gradients that influence plant community composition and physiognomy. Closer to the center of meadows, xeric, shallow soils and greater availability of light at ground level facilitate the persistence of oaks. Although oaks are capable of colonizing these areas, their growth is extremely slow. Moving towards the edge of meadows, slightly decreased sunlight intensity and denser litter layers from surrounding vegetation create more mesic conditions and likely deeper soils. Taller oaks typically occurring in this region of the meadow are probably responding to the more favorable conditions, which at some sites still may be too extreme for potentially competing conifer species. The edge of meadows seems to represent a current environmental threshold where nonoak species, primarily Douglas-fir, are able to persist. Oaks also occur at this edge but, due to decreased light availability and possibly continuing increases in conifer abundance, they often have smaller crowns and sparse leaf cover, with boles and limbs bending into the available light of the meadow.

These small, xeric locations may represent a refuge for oaks within the conifer-dominated landscape. While oaks in more mesic sites were often overtopped, the poor quality of these sites may permit oak growth to

be "stable and self-perpetuating" (Thilenius 1968; Lorimer 1993 and references therein). In certain communities of the northern oak woodlands in California, Oregon white oak is found in "scrub" form with shallow soils and rocky forested openings (Griffin 1977, Barnhart et al. 1987). Succession on these "poor" quality sites in California, which are also often dominated by grasses, is much slower compared to the typical oak woodlands of the Willamette Valley (Griffin 1977). Barnhart et al. (1987) note that a few foresters in northern California question the ability of Douglas-fir to survive at marginal sites such as these meadows; during drought years conifer species may lose access to water in the shallow soils and succumb to insect attack or branch cankers. A few large Douglas-firs were observed in the center of meadows; however, a number of younger individuals in similar locations showed evidence of needle loss. The current state of these sites suggests that succession to conifer forest is possible but will occur at a very slow rate, if at all.

Woodland-Type Sites

Environmental conditions in woodland-type sites, which were less extreme and less favorable for continued oak dominance, permitted much more potential for change in the canopy composition. The age of the oaks in these small woodlands suggests that they represent species that were capable of expanding into these seasonally wet and drier areas, which where formerly more open. However, as in the closed-form oak stands of the Willamette Valley, the environmental conditions created by the increased oak densities have permitted the initiation of succession to conifer forest. The canopy composition typical of woodland-type sites (Figure 3) depicts an oak stand dominated by closed-form oaks in midcanopy positions with scattered conifers in the upper and lower canopy layers, which will likely slowly succeed the slower growing oaks. This form of succession is also occurring in some very small areas outside of the xeric soils at meadow-type sites where conditions permit conifer growth.

Although this type of succession is more typical of woodland-type sites in the Willamette Valley, the similarity may only reflect the relatively recent increases in oak density and formation of dense oak woodlands resulting from fire suppression. At forested oak stands in the Willamette Valley, Thilenius (1968) regularly found two-aged stands with a minimum of one "relict" oak greater than 40 inches dbh per acre. This represents the xmaximum number of oaks per acre of this size observed during the surveys. The absence of relic trees, large snags, and stumps suggests that conditions at these sites may not have been similar to the pre-European settlement oak savanna Thilenius (1968) describes for the Willamette Valley.

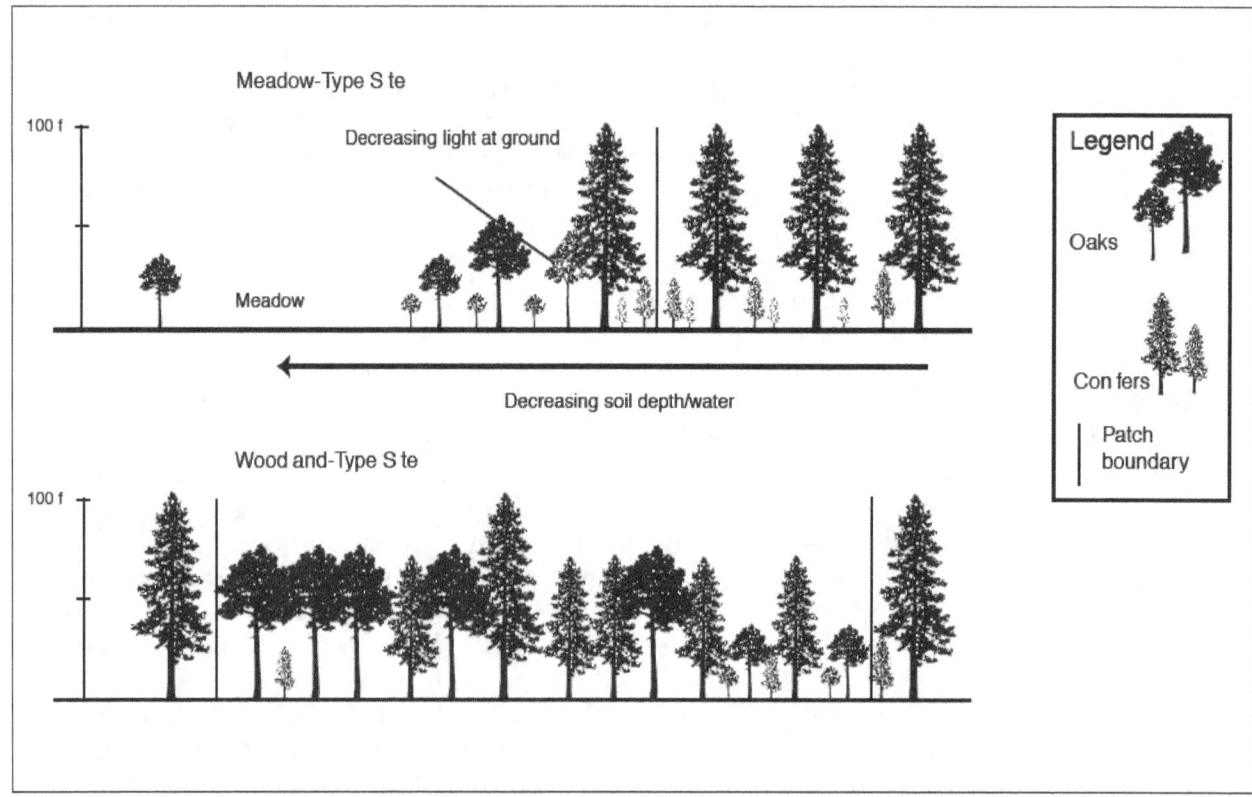

Figure 3. Typical spatial pattern of oaks and conifers in meadow and woodland sites. Hypothetical environmental gradients influencing tree distribution in meadow sites are also shown.

ASSESSMENT OF OAK WOODLAND RESOURCES IN BLM'S EUGENE DISTRICT

Effects of Fire Suppression

The primary causes attributed to the alteration of oak woodlands in the Willamette Valley and surrounding areas include suppression of fire, removal of oaks for fuel and urban development, and grazing practices that alter soil conditions (Johannessen et al. 1971; Towle 1982). Because the surveyed sites were generally isolated from urban disturbances and virtually no evidence of grazing and cutting of oaks was found, changes in fire frequency have potentially had the greatest effect on these oak woodlands.

The frequent and very extensive burning of the Willamette Valley prairies by Native Americans documented by early explorers and settlers (Johannessen et al. 1971) must have reached well into neighboring hills and valleys (Cole 1977). Natural fires may have also been frequent in the Western Cascades, particularly in drier areas (Morrison and Swanson 1990).

Thilenius (1968) has described the effects of postsettlement fire regime on Willamette Valley oak stands. He found that in the former oak savannas and prairies, younger forest-form oaks had started growing near the time when both natural and human induced fires began to be suppressed, following the large immigration of Euro-Americans in the 1840's. A similar trend of increased densities of oaks and other species <150 years old would be expected in oak woodlands in neighboring areas where fires also regulated plant communities.

The mean age estimated for forest-form, cored trees on BLM woodland-type sites (164 years) suggests that the majority of these closed-crown stands also originated at the time of European settlement. Large and older open-form oaks, snags, and decaying logs were very rare or absent. Although there were only a few signs of oak harvesting, it is possible that the lack of snags and larger trees was due in part to past removal. In some sites, fallen snags may have also been very decayed and were not detected during surveys.

Wildlife Habitat Associations

Species That Use Oak Woodlands

Most of the available data on wildlife use of oak woodlands in the West comes from California. According to Ryan and Carey (1995a), there are 331 terrestrial vertebrate species that use oak woodlands, including 120 mammals, 147 birds, and 60 herpetofauna; Barrett (1980) suggested that at least 60 mammal species use oaks; Block and Morrison (1998) found 19 species of herpetofauna; and 110 bird species were recorded using oak habitats by Verner (1980) in California. Gumtow-Farrior and Gumtow-Farrior (1992) listed 214 vertebrates that nest and forge in Oregon oak woodlands. Hagar and Stern (1997) observed 77 bird species using oak woodlands in the Willamette Valley, including 43 residents, 29 migrants and 3 exotic species. Pacific Wildlife Research (1998), using similar study sites in Oregon, found 15 herpetofauna, including 2 salamanders, 1 newt, 4 frogs, 3 lizards, and 3 snake species. Studies on oak woodlands in Oregon are limited because of their limited distribution in a state dominated by coniferous forests. Appendix A provides a list of wildlife species that are most likely to use oak woodlands in Lane County, Oregon.

The following species appear to be associated with oak woodlands or some component of oak-dominated communities and have distributions in Lane County, Oregon. Most of these species may occur in other types of plant communities, but when oaks are present, they rely on them. There are other species that could be considered oak woodland-associated based the definition used for this assessment, and there would probably be many others if information on habitat utilization of oak woodlands was available.

Deer

The extent to which deer use oaks can be particularly heavy, and when acorns are available during the fall and winter seasons, they are the primary food source of the white-tailed deer (*Odocoileus virginianus*) in oak woodlands (Christisen and Korschgen 1955). Menke and Fry (1980) examined rumen contents of 61 black-tailed deer (*Odocoileus hemionus columbianus*) in California and found year-round consumption of oak browse (twigs and leaves) averaged 21.5 percent of their diet per month. The highest seasonal consumption they found was in the summer when oak browse and acorns accounted for 60 percent of their diet. Acorns alone constituted 15-20 percent of their diet in the summer and fall (Menke and Fry 1980). Similarly, monthly consumption of acorns ranged from 0 percent in June to 62.4 percent in October, and averaged 25.2 percent per month over a period of 6 years (Christisen and Korschgen 1955). Coblentz (1980) found 48 percent of the stomach contents of four black-tailed deer were comprised of acorns in the Willamette Valley, Oregon. Studies throughout the United States have found similar results for deer (Pearson and Burnett 1940; Forbes et al. 1941; Sanders 1941; Pearson 1943; Halloran 1943; Taylor 1944; Dalke 1947; Dexter et al. 1952; Lay 1957; Collins 1961; Duvendeck 1962; Lay 1965). Acorns are a high-energy source of food and have a strong influence on reproduction, survival, and population levels of deer in a given year (Nichol 1938; Forbes et al. 1941; Duvendeck 1962).

Sharptail Snake

In part because of its limited distribution, especially in Oregon, the sharptail snake (*Contia tenuis*) has been designated as "sensitive and vulnerable" (SV) by the Oregon Department of Fish and Wildlife (Marshall et al. 1996). Cook (1960) described specific accounts of the species in California and Oregon, most in close proximity to oaks. Applegarth (1994) suggested that sharptail snakes are found in open oak woodlands mixed with madrone and chinkapin, with <40 percent canopy cover and with a grass, forb, brush understory, often accompanied by poison oak. Cook (1960) suggested the distribution of sharptail snakes might be limited by their specific food preference of small slugs. In contrast, Applegarth (1994) suggested that habitat loss of oak/grass woodlands due to cattle grazing and conversion to Douglas-fir forests have limited the distribution of sharptail snake populations. The sharptail snake is considered rare in Lane County (Applegarth 1994). However, the BLM oak patch sites sampled are very similar to those considered as good sharptail snake habitat.

Wild Turkey

Wild turkeys (*Meleagris gallopavo*) have been introduced in Oregon and are found in oak woodlands and oak-conifer habitats. Their diet includes seeds, nuts, grains, buds, leaves, arthropods, and some vertebrate species, but acorns are a preferred food in winter when they are available. Wild turkey acorn consumption has been found to continue throughout all or most of the year in many areas (Christisen and Korschgen 1955; Good and Webb 1940; May et al. 1939; Mosby and Handley 1943). Monthly percentage of total volume of acorns consumed ranged from 0.5 percent in September to 73.3 percent in January and averaged 22.7 percent per month in Missouri (Christisen and Korschgen 1955). Similar studies reported heavy utilization of acorns by wild turkeys (Good and Webb 1940; Ligon 1946; May et al. 1939; Mosby and Handley 1943). Uhlig and Bailey (1952) suggested wild turkey mortality rates were associated with low mast production in West Virginia. Smith and Browning (1967) found that grass seed was the primary staple of wild turkeys in oak woodland chaparral habitat in California, with acorns being only a secondary source in the fall. They suggested that competition for food (from cattle and other birds), rather than the food source itself, may be a potential limiting factor to turkeys in California.

Acorn Woodpecker

The acorn woodpecker (*Melanerpes formicivorus*), unlike most other oak woodland associates, is specifically restricted to habitats that have some oak component, whether they are oak woodlands or oak-pine forests. Acorn woodpeckers feed primarily on insects, small vertebrates, wild oaks, fruit, oak buds and flowers, and acorns (Koenig 1980). Koenig (1980) stated that stored acorns are often used year-round, but most importantly in September-March, and MacRoberts and MacRoberts (1976) suggested acorn woodpecker winter diets in California consisted almost entirely of acorns. Koenig (1978) and Hannon et al. (1987) suggested that populations and reproduction are limited by the availability of an adequate supply of stored acorns during the more crucial winter months. Similarly, Koenig and Mumme (1987) found that reproductive success, clutch size, population dynamics, and winter survival rates of the acorn woodpecker were all determined by the available supply of stored acorns. Koenig (1980) estimated that stored acorns account for only about 6-7 percent of the total annual metabolic requirements of acorn woodpeckers. According to Wilson et al. (1991), the dbh of granary trees selected by acorn woodpeckers was significantly larger than nongranary trees, and they suggested that acorn woodpecker populations are limited by the availability of large >30 inches dbh oaks. They also suggested acorn woodpeckers are important as the primary excavators for secondary cavity nesters in oak woodlands. Wilson et al. (1991) suggested management that maintains large oaks (>20 inches dbh) to benefit the entire cavity nesting guild.

Western Gray Squirrel

Western gray squirrel (*Sciurus griseus*) distribution in Oregon and Washington is mostly in conifer-hardwood forests with a strong component of Oregon white oak (Cross 1969), and the forests they inhabit usually have some species of oak present (Asserson 1974; Cross 1969; Foster 1992; Gilman 1986). The squirrel is listed as "sensitive-undermined" by the Oregon Department of Fish and Wildlife (Marshall et al. 1996). Acorns and conifer seeds are a primary component of their summer-winter diet in California, Oregon, and Washington (Asserson 1974; Barnum 1975; Cross 1969; Foster 1992; Stienecker and Browning 1970), but fungi, fruits, buds, and leafy vegetation are also important (Byrne 1979; Foster 1992; Maser et al. 1978; Ryan and Carey 1995a; Stienecker and Browning 1970). Ryan and Carey (1995b) found western gray squirrels were positively associated with food-producing shrubs including snowberry, California hazel, bigleaf maple (*Acer macrophyllum*), vine maple (*Acer circinatum*), salal (*Gaultheria shallon*), and blackberries, and negatively associated with Scotch broom. The high-energy content of mast foods, in addition to their ability to stay fresh when stored for use during more critical months when other food availability is low, makes them a superior food source during some seasons of the year (Stienecker and Browning 1970). Ryan and Carey (1995a) suggested oaks may be the single most important source of food for western gray squirrels; however, annual mast production by oak species can be highly variable (Beck 1993) and acorns are an unpredictable source of food for wildlife. Western gray squirrels must rely on other foods, including seeds, buds, and stems from other trees; fungi; and forbs during years when the acorn crop is low or has failed (Ryan and Carey 1995a). Ryan and Carey (1995a) suggested two of the most limiting factors of western gray squirrel abundance are the availability of oak-dominated habitats and the availability of mast, and they suggested that management for western gray squirrels include a minimum of 18 ft^2 basal area of

oaks. They predicted that the minimum size required for oak stands to support western gray squirrels was 2-3 acres for short-term usage and >5 acres to support long-term requirements.

Dusky-Footed Woodrat, Common Bushtit, Scrub Jay, White-Breasted Nuthatch, and Mourning Dove

Information on these remaining oak woodland-associated species, the dusky-footed woodrat (*Neotoma fuscipes*), common bushtit (*Psaltriparus minimus*), scrub jay (*Aphelocoma caerulescens*), white-breasted nuthatch (*Sitta carolinensis*), and mourning dove (*Zenaida macroura*), is limited to more generalized group studies instead of species-specific assessments of habitat utilization of oak woodlands. A combination of these studies and information on the ecology and habits of each species from the literature was used to categorize them as oak woodland associates.

Habitat Components of Oak Woodlands

Food

Acorns are an important high-energy food resource to many wildlife species in oak woodlands (Block et al. 1990; Pavlik et al. 1991; Kerns 1980; Goodrum et al. 1971; Christisen and Korschgen 1955; Martin et al. 1951). Acorns are an important seasonal source of energy prior to the harsh winter months when other foods are less abundant or nutritious (Block et al. 1990), and are used year-round by some species that cache the surplus (Goodrum 1940; Good and

Webb 1940). Christisen and Korschgen (1955) listed deer, turkeys, quail, ducks, and crows as species that rely heavily on acorns for food during parts of the year. Some experts suggested that at least 37 species of terrestrial mammals and 30 birds eat acorns in oak woodlands in California (Block et al. 1990). Acorn availability is important for the survival, reproductive success, and population size of many oak woodland species (Forbes et al. 1941; Linduska 1950; Burns et al. 1954; Uhlig 1956; Duvendeck 1962). Van Dersal (1940) suggested that the distribution of some wildlife species may be associated with the range of oak habitat, and Coblentz (1980) suggested that acorn loss by oak removal would have detrimental effects on local populations of some species in the Willamette Valley. Goodrum et al. (1971) suggested that freezing temperatures resulted in acorn crop failure during 1 year of their study, and Sharp and Sprague (1967) found 4 years with total crop failure and partial crop failure in 4 other years over a 50-year period due to freezing temperatures. In addition to weather, Block et al. (1990) listed genetics, nutrition, close proximity to other trees causing root crowding and shading, soil conditions, and physiographical features as variables that may affect acorn production. The negative impact of acorn crop failure on some wildlife populations can be devastating. For example, Christisen and Korschgen (1955) suggested that there was a direct correlation with gray squirrel abundance and the abundance of acorns, and population levels of gray squirrels, bears, pigs, and deer may be limited by the annual crop of acorn mast (Goodrum 1940; Duvendeck 1962; Piekielek and Burton 1975; Barrett 1978).

Oak foliage and plant species associated with oaks are another important food source to wildlife in oak woodlands. Kerns (1980) found wildlife species diversity and abundance was associated with the density of understory plants in northern California oak habitats. Block et al. (1990) suggested that the majority of wildlife in California oak habitats depend on the fruit from plants associated with oak woodlands. Some of the more common fruit bearing shrubs in California oak woodlands include: redberry (*Rhamnus crocea*), coffeeberry (*R. californicus*), buckbrush (*Ceanothus cuneatus*), toyon (*Heteromeles arbutifolia*) and mistletoe (*Phoradendron* spp.) (Block et al. 1990; Block and Morrison 1991). Manzanita and mistletoe and other species of *Ceanothus* may provide food resources for animals in Oregon oak woodlands. Kerns (1980) compared mature oak, mixed oak-conifer, young oak, and oak conifer edge habitats in northern California and found that the mature oak habitats with dense understory of shrubs and grasses were highest for species diversity and abundance of wildlife. Kerns suggested that the fruit, seeds, stems, and leaves from shrubs, combined with the niche created by the vertical edge between the shrub layer and the mature oak canopy, produce desirable habitat for a variety of wildlife species.

Cover

According to Ingles (1965), Barrett et al. (1976), and Pavlik et al. (1991), oaks provide an important source of cover from exposure for mammals in California. The combination of trees and shrubs in oak woodlands provides a vertical structure that helps conceal mammal den sites and prey from predators and provides habitat for many shrub nesting bird species (Pavlik et al. 1991). Leaf litter, grass and forb cover, and coarse woody debris are important cover variables to herpetofauna in California oak woodlands (Block and Morrison 1998). Cavities in standing or fallen oak trees and snags are used for nesting, estivation, and protection from predators by many amphibian and reptile species; in addition, there is a diverse community of bird species that nest in oak canopies and others that rely on cavities for nesting (Pavlik et al. 1991). Verner (1983) suggested that oak woodlands were among the top three habitat types in North America for breeding bird diversity. Hagar and Stern (1997) found more neotropical migrants breeding in oak woodlands in the Willamette Valley than others have found in Douglas-fir forests in western Oregon (Carey et al. 1991; McGarigal and McComb 1992), and many of the more common resident species they found were rare or absent from closed canopy Douglas-fir forests. Wilson et al. (1991) found 6 of the 10 most abundant breeding birds in California oak woodlands were cavity nesters. Cavity nesters comprised 25 percent of the breeding species and more than 58 percent of the total individuals breeding in their study, which they suggested is higher than densities of most other bird communities in temperate regions.

Restoration and Management Literature Review

Conifer Encroachment

Intensive efforts to restore Oregon white oak woodlands have been conducted at two public parks in Northern California: Redwood National Park and Annadel State Park. Literature on similar restoration studies in oak woodlands of the Pacific Northwest was not located at the time of this review.

Oak woodlands in Redwood National Park are known as bald hills oak woodlands, which are characterized by a patchy mosaic of oak- and grass-dominated areas (Reed and Sugihara 1987). Suppression of frequent fires (both natural and those set by Native Americans) is believed to have led to increased oak densities since the 1850's (Reed and Sugihara 1987), forming more even-aged stands and more narrow-crowned trees. Douglas-fir encroachment has noticeably decreased the extent of prairie and oak woodland (Sugihara and Reed 1987b).

In order to achieve the park's goals of managing and restoring these oak woodlands, various prescribed burns have been carried out (Sugihara and Reed 1987a, 1987b). When sufficient fuels occurred in areas to be burned, low-intensity backing and head fires killed nearly all Douglas-firs <9 feet and larger Douglas-firs that were very scorched (70 percent scorching of trees or greater) (Sugihara and Reed 1987b). These fires also top-killed most oaks <9 feet; however, these individuals sprouted back in the following years. Larger oaks, >9 feet, were generally unharmed and also produced basal sprouts following the fires. Less intense fires (fires remaining in the understory) were unable to kill trees >9 feet.

Sugihara and Reed (1987a) concluded that in order to successfully control Douglas-fir growth, fire frequency would need to occur at least every 10 years. They have also suggested that creating a multiaged stand of oaks, typical of pre-European settlement in this area, would require low-intensity fire at intervals of approximately 5 years. In the bald hills of Redwood National Park, regular low-intensity fires would likely decrease the damage to canopy trees while lowering the constant regeneration from previous fires. In addition, sustained burning may restore other native vegetation adapted to frequent fires.

Sugihara and Reed (1987a) have also recommended combining prescribed burning with manual removal and/or girdling of larger invasive trees that will not be effectively controlled by fire. Girdled trees may also provide snags for wildlife species.

Studies and work conducted at Annadel State Park in the Sonoma Mountains of California have focused on describing the causes of Douglas-fir invasion and restoration strategies for oak woodlands at this park (Barnhart et al. 1987; Barnhart et al. 1996; Hastings et al. 1997).

Restoration work of oak woodlands at Annadel State Park has included both manual removal of Douglas-fir and prescribed burning of portions of the park (Hastings et al. 1997). Initial efforts included a combination of prescribed burning in "high priority areas" along with two cutting treatments for Douglas-fir trees >6 inches dbh: 1) application of glyphosate to shallow cuts in the cambium layer of larger Douglas-firs, and 2) felling of smaller trees, which added fuel for burn areas. Trained volunteers later repeated manual removal using the frill cuts without herbicide treatment. Additional prescribed burns were conducted in larger areas (95-242 acres) and monitored to assess survival and regeneration.

Hastings et al. (1997) reported that Douglas-firs receiving the herbicide treatments were killed; however, recruitment of this species continued in areas where large trees were left standing and numerous smaller felled trees were able to sprout from stumps left too high. Additional cuts without herbicide were effective; however, some trees >12 inches dbh survived, likely due to shallow cuts.

Prescribed burning was effective in decreasing the number of Douglas-fir seedlings per acre by 50 percent, while Oregon white oak seedlings increased by 9 percent. Areas of native California fescue grasses (Festuca californica) burned with high intensity, while areas with less surface fuels permitted survival of Douglas-fir seedlings.

Because prescribed burning is not effective in all areas, current management strategies at this park include using a combination of burning and manual removal of seedlings where burning is not as effective (Hastings et al. 1997).

Thinning of Closed-Canopy Stands

McDonald and Ritchie (1994) have suggested that thinning of California black oak stands may be beneficial for wildlife by allowing trees to produce larger crowns, leading to increased acorn production. However, they point out that thinning of this species often results in the formation of epicormic branches that yield no acorns. These small subcrown branches are produced by less vigorous trees often occurring in closed canopy stands. McDonald and Ritchie suggest that a series of thinnings will allow the trees to gradually increase in vigor, and thus crown size, and reduce the rate of epicormic branching.

Tappeiner and McDonald (1980) note that for California black oak, although acorn production generally increases after 80 years, the incidence of heart rot also increases at this time. Therefore they suggest that the availability of acorns may be more continuous in oak woodlands if two broad age classes of trees (0-80 and 81-120+ years) are maintained. Because mast production often varies among trees at individual sites (Beck 1993), identifying and retaining better producing trees may also increase the availability of acorns for wildlife.

Vegetation Patterns

The vegetation structure and spatial distribution of oaks is highly variable among the 13 BLM sites surveyed. From a landscape perspective, all of the sites represented small patches of oaks (median area = 2 acres) imbedded in a heterogeneous mosaic of conifer stands, clearcuts, and non-forested areas. However, some BLM sites (e.g., Cougar Mountain, Gilkey Creek, Sears Road) represented only a portion of a larger oak-conifer woodland extending outside of the surveyed patch boundaries. The relatively small patches of oaks delineated do not adequately represent the structural or compositional richness of the plant communities observed at the BLM sites. The spatial distribution of oaks often appeared to be influenced by environmental gradients (i.e., soil moisture, aspect), and oak trees were frequently interspersed among conifers and other hardwood species. Oaks that are able to persist among conifers in canopy gaps or along stand edges provided a unique structural component in the vertical stratification of these stands. Arboreal lichens, other epiphytes, and nonvascular plants associated with oaks are likely to increase the plant species diversity at the BLM sites to a much greater extent than the presence of oak as a single tree species would indicate.

Much of the variation in oak distribution observed on the BLM sites appears to be influenced by interactions among aspect, slope position, and soil characteristics that influence microclimate and soil moisture. Oak trees tended to be most highly aggregated on xeric, south- or southwest-facing hill slopes or ridges that were less favorable to conifer reproduction. On the most extreme sites, even oaks are infrequent and the sites are dominated by grass or shrubs. It remains unclear whether oaks will eventually infiltrate these meadows and dominate the site; it may be that these areas are so prone to drought that tree establishment is unlikely to ever occur. In general, oak regeneration was not abundant and most commonly observed in areas where light levels were relatively high; i.e., meadows and light gaps in woodland-type patches. Most of this regeneration was vegetative sprouting, which formed the clusters of shrub-form oaks characteristic of meadow-type patches. Live oak trees rarely were observed to have crowns in dominant canopy positions on mesic sites, although decadent oaks interspersed among conifers or big-leaf maples occurred at a few sites.

These observations may indicate that most of the BLM sites situated on xeric, mid- to upper-slope positions are likely to have oak trees in dominant or codominant canopy positions, regardless of fire suppression (assuming no tree harvest). However, there is evidence (e.g., oak snags under conifer canopies, Douglas-fir seedlings/saplings under oaks) that Douglas-fir are becoming more abundant on mesic sites and dominating stands that had been oak-conifer woodlands and savannas. Based on these observations at the BLM sites and a review of vegetation studies conducted in the Willamette Valley and foothills of the Cascades, it appears that the cessation of perennial fires by Native Americans and active fire suppression has promoted conifer succession on all but the driest sites.

Vegetation maps of Lane County constructed from surveys performed in the 1850's indicate that the BLM McKenzie and South Valley Resource Areas were a heterogeneous landscape of Douglas-fir forest, mixed conifer-hardwood forest, Oregon white oak-ponderosa pine forest, mixed species savanna, and prairie. Most of the BLM sites surveyed appear to have been closed-canopy forest or woodland plant communities at the time of European settlement in this area (Table 13). However, notes from the historic surveys suggest that tree densities were lower and average tree diameter in these stands may have been greater than the 1998 estimates. Retrospective studies (Johannessen et al. 1971; Cole 1977) and the 1850's surveys also indicate that ponderosa pine was commonly associated with oaks in this area and probably much more extensively distributed in the Willamette Valley foothills than it is today.

Some federal planners and ecologists have recommended that natural forests serve as a reference to guide desired composition and structure of forest reserves (Dombeck 1996; Thomas 1996; Swanson et al. 1997). If oak woodlands such as those surveyed are to be managed in this way:

❖ The diversity of tree species should be sustained: although there is no data

available to fully examine the variation of forest composition prior to European settlement, the 1850's surveys suggest that much of the McKenzie and South Valley Resource Areas were mixed stands of Douglas-fir, ponderosa pine, and Oregon white oak.

❖ The importance of meadows, canopy gaps, and rocky balds should be recognized: these relatively small openings are relatively undisturbed (compared to adjacent pastures and clearcuts) and may be important strongholds for native, early seral plants, reptiles, and small mammals.

To help determine possible management or restoration actions, the 13 surveyed sites were classified into three groups based on site characteristics and the degree of oak-conifer competition observed (Table 14):

❖ Xeric: Dry sites on ridges or steep, south-to-southwest hill slopes have limited oak size and conifer growth in these sites, which have likely undergone the least amount of change in community structure post-European settlement.

❖ Mesic: Lower slopes and increased patch cover by more mesic soils in these sites have provided more favorable growing conditions and thus greater and more rapid changes in canopy composition over time relative to xeric sites.

❖ Wet: Sites occurring on low slopes where mesic and seasonally wet soils covered >50 percent of the patch area have undergone the most dramatic changes in canopy composition. Within the last 150 years, closed-canopy oak and mixed conifer stands have developed to cover the majority of these formerly more open areas.

Table 13. Historical vegetation classifications for the surveyed sites. Classifications are taken from GIS maps created from interpretative data of Christy et al. (1996, 1997). A dashed line in the table indicates that information was not available for that location.

Site	Major Vegetation Classification	Specific Vegetation Classification
Anthony Creek	Closed forest upland	-
Bates	Woodland	Scattering or thinly timbered Douglas-fir/white oak (bigleaf maple) woodland, with brushy undergrowth of hazel, other shrubs, oak brush, oak stump sprouts, young Douglas-fir, bracken, briars, and sometimes willow.
Cougar Mountain	Prairie, closed forest upland	-
Eagle's Nest	-	-
Fox Hollow	-	Mixture of 1) xeric Douglas-fir/Chinquapin-madrone forest on south slopes 2) mesic Douglas-fir/bigleaf maple forest on north slopes and bottoms, sometimes with incense cedar, oak, grand fir, red cedar, yew, red alder and dogwood.
Gilkey Creek	Closed forest upland bordering savanna and prairie	Bordering areas: Oregon white oak/Douglas-fir/ponderosa pine savanna and white oak/ponderosa pine savanna.
Kloster Mountain	-	-
Rattlesnake Butte	Woodland and closed forest upland	-
Sears Road	Prairie	-
Seventy-Ninth	Closed forest upland	-
Weiss Road	Woodland	Scattering or thinly timbered Douglas-fir/white oak (bigleaf maple) woodland, with brushy undergrowth of hazel, other shrubs, oak brush, oak stump sprouts, young Douglas-fir, bracken, briars, and sometimes willow.
Wendling	-	Mixture of 1) xeric Douglas-fir/Chinquapin-madrone forest on south slopes 2) mesic Douglas-fir/bigleaf maple forest on north slopes and bottoms, sometimes with incense cedar, oak, grand fir, red cedar, yew, red alder and dogwood.
Wills Road	Woodland and closed forest upland	-

Table 14. Classification of surveyed sites based on site characteristics, degree of conifer competition, and possible management actions.

Site Groupings (M =meadow community type; W =woodland community type)	Environmental Conditions and Oak Growth and Distribution Characteristics	Possible Ecosystem Management or Restoration Actions
Xeric Anthony Creek (M) Bates (could also be in mesic group) (M) Kloster Mountain (M)	- dry, steep slopes - low soil moisture levels - oaks typically shrubby and short (< 40 feet) with thin stems	- protect meadows by controlling increase of nonnative plant cover - monitor and eliminate future conifer encroachment
Mesic Fox Hollow (W) (could also be in wet group) Gilkey Creek (M) Rattlesnake (M) Seventy-Ninth (M) Wendling (M) Weiss Road (M	- medium slopes - low to medium soil moisture levels - open areas with small shrubby or stunted oaks - woodland areas with larger oaks (30-60 feet) typically overtopped by conifers to some degree	- sustain and/or restore diversity of tree species, particularly ponderosa pine and Oregon white oak - control nonnative plants - historic vegetation classifications may provide reference conditions - possible silvicultural methods include thinning of conifers and smaller oaks; snag creation
Wet Cougar Mountain (W) Eagle's Rest (W) Sears Road (W) Wills Road (W)	- low slope areas - medium to high seasonal soil moisture levels - large (60-80 feet) forest form oaks; only a few older open grown trees with conifer encroachment very evident	- restoration of open woodlands, prairie, savanna will require intensive, susained efforts - eliminate/control abundant nonnative plants - silvicultural treatments may include selective thinning of oaks and conifers; prescribed burning; snag creation

Wildlife Habitat

Mast Production

Goodrum et al. (1971) studied the relationship between acorn production and tree characteristics of seven oak species in Texas and Louisiana. He found acorn yields generally increased with age, bole diameter, and crown size of the tree. Similarly, Christisen and Korschgen (1955) found a strong association between crown size and acorn production. In contrast, Cypert (1951) suggested radial growth rate rather than tree size was the most important factor determining the size of the acorn crop. The BLM oak patches were not directly samples for acorn production because of time and logistic constraints; however, expected acorn yields for white oak (*Q. alba*) from Goodrum et al. (1971) were used to calculate acorn potential production rates using tree dimensions from the BLM oak patches. Potential acorn yield based on numbers of oak trees in acorn producing size classes from each of the BLM patches ranged from 0 to 1,333 total pounds per oak patch (mean = 195 pounds), and from 0 to 494 pounds of acorns per acre (mean = 89 pounds) (Table 15). Sixteen of 25 oak patch sites were predicted to yield less than 50 pounds/acre of acorns, including 10 that were predicted to have less than 10 pounds/acre. The four highest yields were >250 pounds/acre. The reason the estimated yields were lower than might be expected given the number of trees in some of the oak patches is that most of the oaks were <15 inches dbh, which is at the smaller end of the size found to produce acorns by Goodrum et al. (1971). Although these expected yields are very crude estimates based on a different oak species from a different part of the country, the estimates may be high rather than low because they don't account for the percentage of trees that don't produce acorns and the cyclic nature of mast production. In the Willamette Valley, mast years have occurred very infrequently in the last 15 years (David Hibbs personal communication). Goodrum et al. (1971) also suggested that tree size positively influenced the percentage of trees that produced acorns, and an important limiting factor of acorn production can be freezing winter temperatures. Verner (1980) suggested managing oak woodlands for wildlife should include a minimum of 100 pounds of acorns per acre, which exceeds the approximated acorn yield for 70 percent of the oak patches sampled. Therefore it appears that only the Cougar Mountain, Eagle's Rest, Gilkey Creek, Sears Road, and Wills Road sites might be capable of producing a significant abundance of acorns available for wildlife.

Vegetation

Average shrub coverage ranged from 24 to 65 percent in nine oak woodland sites in the Willamette Valley (Hagar and Stern 1997). Poison oak was the dominant shrub species in four of their sites, and Franklin and Dyrness (1988) stated it to be the dominant shrub species in most oak woodlands in Oregon and Washington. Similarly, poison oak dominated the understory vegetation in the oak patches sampled. In addition, there was a high frequency of nonnative plant occurrence (Table 10). However, in contrast to Hagar and Stern (1997), coverage of other shrub species important to

Table 15. Estimated annual acorn yields for the surveyed patches. Yields were approximated using data from Goodrum et al. (1971; Table 2) and estimated numbers of oak trees in acorn-producing size classes.

Patch	Patch Area (acres)	Total Estimated Acorn Yield (pounds)	Estimated Acorn Yield (pounds/acre)
ANTH-1	1	5.0	5.0
ANTH-2	2	5.0	2.5
ANTH-3	2	5.0	2.5
BATES	3	15.0	5.0
COUG-1	2	550.0	275.0
COUG-2	2	290.0	145.0
EAGL-1	1	495.0	495.0
EAGL-2	2	790.0	395.0
FOX	2	110.0	55.0
GILK-1	2	275.0	135.0
GILK-2	1	35.0	35.0
GILK-3	2	165.0	80.0
KLOS-1	3	5.0	2.5
KLOS-2	3	5.0	2.5
KLOS-3	5	0.0	0.0
KLOS-4	3	15.0	5.0
RATT-1	4	100.0	25.0
RATT-2	3	60.0	20.0
RATT-3	4	90.0	20.0
SEARS	5	1,330.0	265.0
SEVENT	2	35.0	15.0
WEISS	3	150.0	50.0
WEND-1	2	15.0	7.5
WEND-2	3	0.0	0.0
WILLS	2	330.0	165.0
Mean		195.0	88.3

wildlife is much less frequent in the BLM oak patches, and many that were common in their study are rare or absent, including; service berry (*Amelanchier alnifolia*), ootka rose (*Rosa nutkana*), and snowberry. Thilenius suggested that previously grazed areas favor poison oak growth because cattle often avoided it, giving it a competitive advantage over other more palatable shrub species, and according to Longhurst et al. (1979), browsing by livestock and deer may be the primary factor impacting regeneration of oaks in California rangelands. Mellanby (1968), Griffin (1971), and Block et al. (1990) suggested that extensive forging on shrubs and oak seedlings can kill or prevent some plants from regenerating. Grazing by wildlife, well-drained soils, shading from bordering conifer forests, and small patch sizes, probably all contribute to the invasion of nonnative plants and high densities of poison oak.

Cavities

The importance of cavities to wildlife in oak woodlands was discussed earlier. Hagar and Stern (1997) suggested that large-diameter white oak trees grown in open areas in Oregon usually produce a greater number of cavities than the same diameter class would in Douglas-fir forests, and they found three cavity nesters in their study were positively correlated with tree diameter. Similarly, five cavity nesters and one open nester were positively associated with the abundance of large-diameter trees (>20 inches dbh) and the abundance of cavities (Wilson et al. 1991). There were only 4 total oak snags >20 inches dbh and 27 conifer snags found among all 13 BLM study sites. In addition, there were less than 10 live oaks >20 inches dbh found at the sites. All the live large

trees and snags >20 inches dbh located were on only 40 percent of the sites. Consequently, the value of the majority of the oak patch sites to cavity nesting species, especially those associated with larger diameter trees and snags, is poor. Hagar and Stern (1997) suggested that the most limiting factor in the semiopen oak woodlands might be large-diameter oaks for cavity nesting species. Although there were more snags in the smaller size classes found, again the majority of these were concentrated in a few sites. Over 50 percent of all the snags were found on four sites, and over 96 percent were found on just 48 percent of the sites. There were no oak snags found in 68 percent of the oak patch sites. Based on availability of large- and medium-sized snags, it appears that seven of the oak patch sites should provide ample opportunities for cavity nesting species.

Patch Size

Probably the most limiting factor of the oak patch sites, in terms of quality of oak woodland habitat, is their size. Wilson et al. (1991) suggested 50-100 hectares (= ~123-247 acres) as the minimum size of management areas for oak woodlands. These sites would not need to be that large to support populations of some oak woodland associated species; however, they would need to be substantially larger than these patches are. Sisk et al. (1997) reported that composition of avian communities in small oak woodland patches (<3 hectares) in California were primarily driven by the assemblage of birds in the surrounding matrix rather than intrinsic habitat characteristics of the oak patches. An Effective Area Model (EAM) proposed by Sisk et al. (1997) predicts that the influence of matrix on avian community diversity decreases as the ratio of patch interior to perimeter length decreases. Although these data are from oak (species unknown) woodlands in southern California, the results suggest that the BLM sites may be too small to support bird communities that are significantly different than the surrounding conifer forest.

Oak Management Recommendations by Other Authors

Applegarth (1994) included specific recommendations for ecosystem management in areas where the sharptail snake is found: "A) Discourage Douglas-fir trees from replacing the grass/oak community; in the case of a timber sale, leave a 'no-replant' buffer of at least one tree height (50 meters) on all sides of the identified habitat. B) Seems best not to burn identified habitat and probably best not to burn the 'no-replant' buffer. C) Do not compact the soil; do not permit grazing of livestock within forested habitat; do not drive, build roads, or locate skid trails through identified habitat. D) Do not flood or poison habitat."

According to Barrett (1980), wildlife biologists recommend the following for management of oak dependent wildlife: "1) maintain a 25 to 50 percent canopy cover of oaks, 2) maintain a basal area of 200 to 2000 ft^2 per each 40 acres, 3) maintain a mixture of age classes including older, more prolific seeders, and 4) disperse oaks in 0.5-5.0-acre aggregations."

Hagar and Stern (1997) conclude, "Conservation strategies for oak woodlands and their associated assemblages of neotropical-migrant and resident bird species should include the maintenance of large tracts of woodland with minimal edge influence. In addition, a diversity of stand structures will support a diversity of bird species, but species using large-diameter oaks in semi-open woodlands are perhaps the most limited, and should therefore should receive priority consideration in conservation planning."

Verner (1980) recommends the following for birds: "Maintain mixed-species, uneven-aged stands, especially allowing for live oak retention; Provide a continuing supply of oaks, generally distributed on every 1- or 2-acre parcel of the management unit that presently supports oaks; Provide a continuing supply of large, old trees, especially those with a good record of high acorn production; Manage for a mean annual acorn production of at least 100 pounds per acre; Provide an ample shrub layer where one occurs in existing oak stands, and consider the possibility of establishing shrubs in stands from which they were removed in the past; Consider needs of oak-using species from different, adjacent habitat types."

Ryan and Carey (1995a) recommend that management guidelines for oak woodlands in Puget Trough should include the following: "To maximize wildlife use, maintain or develop corridors to link habitat fragments and minimize the adverse impacts of fragmenting the landscape; Retain adjacent stands of conifers and hardwoods; Maintain canopy cover of 40 to 60 percent; Maintain tree species composition at 25-75 percent oak, 25-75 percent Douglas-fir, and 10-20 percent other hardwoods; Preserve a near mix of snags, dead and downed trees, seed trees and den trees; Kill overtopping Douglas-fir to allow oaks to grow to an open form (girdle the Douglas-firs for snag management or fall them to provide coarse woody debris); Thin oak or Douglas-fir/oak stands to reduce over crowding and water stress and allow remaining oaks to become larger, more vigorous, more productive, and more fire resistant; Remove smaller Douglas-fir trees under the oak canopy that are competing with oaks for water and that will eventually overtop the oaks; Retain old-growth Douglas fir within oak stands; Maintain a mix of age and size classes of hardwoods to provide sustained mast production, vertical diversity, and recruitment (Bleier et al. 1993); Plan periodic burns of the grass and shrub layer to stimulate young shoot growth, prevent dense shrub competition (particularly Scotch broom), and maintain tree spacing (Columbia Gorge Audubon Society 1990).; Maintain an open to patchy understory with a high level of vegetation diversity; Minimize human disturbance such as excessive trails and roads which accelerate root damage to oaks and invasion of weedy species."

LITERATURE CITED

Anderson, S.H. 1972. Seasonal variations in forest birds of western Oregon. Northwest Science 46(3):194-206.

Applegarth, J.S. 1994. Special status amphibians and reptiles of the Eugene District–a guide for their conservation. USDI BLM, Eugene District, Oregon.

Asserson, W.C., III. 1974. Western gray squirrel studies in Kern County, California. Sacramento, CA: California Department of Fish and Game; Admin. rep. 74.1. 32 pp.

Barnhart, S.J., J.R. McBride, C. Cicero, P. da Silva, and P. Warner. 1987. Vegetation dynamics of the northern oak woodland. In Plumb, T.R., and N.H. Pillsbury tech. coords. Proceedings of the symposium on multiple-use management of California's hardwood resources, November 12-14, 1986; San Luis Obispo, CA. Gen. Tech. Rep. PSW-100; Pacific Southwest Research Station, Forest Service, USDA.

Barnhart, S.J., J.R McBride, and P. Warner. 1996. Invasion of northern oak woodlands by *Pseudotsuga menziesii* (Mirb.) Franco in the Sonoma Mountains of California. Madrono 43(1): 28-45.

Barnum, D.A. 1975. Aspects of western gray squirrel ecology. Pullman, WA: Washington State University. M.S. thesis. 55 pp.

Barrett, R.H. 1978. The feral hog at the Dye Creek Ranch. Hilgardia 46(9):283-355.

Barrett, R.H. 1980. Mammals of California oak habitats–management implications. In Plumb, T.R., tech. coord. Proceedings of the symposium on the ecology, management, and utilization of California oaks, June 26-28, 1979; Claremont, CA. Gen. Tech Rep. PSW-44; Pacific Southwest Research Station, Forest Service, USDA. 275-291.

Barrett, R.H., J.M. Menke, M.E. Fry, and D. Mangold. 1976. A review of the value of hardwoods to wildlife in California with recommendations for research. A report of research performed for the Tahoe National Forest, USDA. RO Supplement Number 8, Part A under master agreement number 21-395. 45 pp.

Beck, D.E. 1993 Acorns and oak regeneration. In Loftis, D. and C.E. McGee, eds. Proceedings of a symposium on oak regeneration: serious problems, practical solutions, September 8-10; Knoxville, Tennessee. Gen. Tech Rep. SE-84; Ashville, NC; USDA, Forest Service, Southeastern Forest Experiment Station. pp. 96-104.

Bleier, C., C. Bolsinger, L. Huntsinger (and others). 1993. A planner's guide for oak woodlands. In Guisti, G.A and P.J. Tinnin, eds. Integrated hardwood range management program. Berkley, CA: University of California. 94 p.

Block, W.M. and M.L. Morrison. 1991. Influence of scale on the management of wildlife in California oak woodlands. In Standiford, R.B., tech. coord. Proceedings of a symposium on oak woodlands and hardwood rangeland management, October 31-November 2, 1990; Davis, CA. Gen Tech. Rep. PSW-126; Pacific Southwest Research Station, Forest Service, USDA; pp. 96-104.

Block, W.M. and M.L. Morrison. 1998. Habitat relationships of amphibians and reptiles in California woodlands. Journal of Herpetology 32(1):51-60.

Block W.M., M.L. Morrison, and J. Verner. 1990. Wildlife and oak-woodland interdependency. Fremontia 18(3): 72-76.

Brown, E.R. (tech. ed.). 1985. Management of wildlife and fish habitats in forests of western Oregon and Washington. USDA Forest Service, Publication Number R6-F&WL-1921985, Portland, OR.

Burns, P.Y., D.M. Christisen, and J.M. Nichols. 1954. Acorn production in the Missouri Ozarks. Univ. of Missouri Agr. Exp. Sta. Tech. Bull. 611. 8 pp.

Byrne, S. 1979. The distribution and ecology of the non-native tree squirrels *Sciurus carolinensis* and *Sciurus niger* in northern California. Berkeley, CA: University of California. Ph.D. dissertation. 196 pp.

Cadwell, C. 1998. GIS application for vegetation and land management treatment tracking. BLM, Eugene District, Oregon.

Carey, A.B., M.M. Hardt, S.P. Horton, and B.L. Biswell. 1991. Spring bird communities in the Oregon Coast Range. In Ruggiero, K.B., A.B. Carey, and M.H. Huff, tech. coords. Wildlife and vegetation and unmanaged Douglas-fir forests. U.S. For. Ser. Gen. Tech. Rep. PNW-285. pp. 123-142.

Christisen, D.M. and L.J. Korschgen. 1955. Acorn yields and wildlife usage in Missouri. Proc. North Am Wildl. Conf. 20:337-357.

Christy, J., M.P. Dougherty, and S.C. Kolar. 1996. Interpretation of transcriptions of general land office survey data. Unpublished report. Oregon Natural Heritage Program. The Nature Conservancy of Oregon. 8 pp.

Christy, J.A., E.R. Alverson, M.P. Dougherty, and S.C. Kolar. 1997. Provisional classification of "presettlement" vegetation in Oregon, as recorded by general land office surveyors. Unpublished report. Oregon Natural Heritage Program. The Nature Conservancy of Oregon. 9 pp.

Coblentz, B.E. 1980. Production of Oregon white oak acorns in the Willamette Valley, Oregon. Wildlife Society Bulletin 8(4):348-350.

Cole, D. 1977. Ecosystem dynamics in the coniferous forest of the Willamette Valley, Oregon, U.S.A. Journal of Biogeography 4(2):181-192.

Collins, J.O. 1961. Ten year acorn mast production study in Louisiana. Louisiana Wildlife and Fisheries Comm. P-R Rept., Project W-29-R-8. 33 pp.

Columbia Gorge Audubon Society. 1990. A plan for managing oak forests of Washington State. Hood River, OR: Columbia Gorge Audubon Society. 36 pp.

Cook, S.F. 1960. On the occurrence and life history of *Contia tenuois*. Herpetologica 16:163-173.

Cross, S.P. 1969. Behavioral aspects of western gray squirrel ecology. Tucson, AZ: University of Arizona. Ph.D. dissertation. 168 pp.

Csuti, B., A.J. Kimerling, T.A. O'Neil, M.M. Shaughnessy, E.P. Gaines, M.M.P. Huso. 1997. Atlas of Oregon wildlife. Oregon State University Press. Corvallis, Oregon. 492 pp.

Cypert, E. 1951. Suggestions for the management of oak forests for mast production. Presented at the Southeastern Assoc. Game and Fish Commissioners Conf. 8 pp.

Dalke, P.D. 1947. Deer foods in the Missouri Ozarks. Missouri Conservationist 8(9):4-5.

Dexter, R.W., S.J. Cortese and S.A. Reed. 1952. An analysis of food habits of the white-tailed deer. Ohio Wildlife Management 5(1):34-39.

Dombeck, M.P. 1996. Thinking like a mountain: BLM's approach to ecosystem management. Ecological Applications 6(3): 699-702.

Duvendeck, J.P. 1962. The value of acorns in the diet of Michigan deer. Journal of Wildlife Management 26(4): 371-379.

Forest Ecosystem Management Team (FEMAT). 1993. Forest ecosystem management: an ecological, economic, and social assessment. Portland, OR; U.S. Department of Agriculture; U.S. Department of the Interior (and others).

Forbes, E.B., L.F. Marcy, A.L. Voris, and C.E. French. 1941. The digestive capacities of white-tailed deer. Journal of Wildlife Management 5(1):108-114.

Foster, S.A. 1992. Studies of ecological factors that effect the population and distribution of the western gray squirrel in north central Oregon. Portland, OR: Portland State University. Ph.D. dissertation. 154 pp.

Franklin, J.F. and C.T. Dyrness. 1988. Natural vegetation of Oregon and Washington. Oregon State University Press, Corvallis, Oregon. 452 pp.

Gilman, K.N. 1986. The western gray squirrel (*Sciurus griseus*), its summer home range, activity times, and habitat usage in Northern California. Sacramento, CA: California State University. M.S. thesis. 71 pp.

Good, H.G. and L.G. Webb. 1940. Spring foods of the wild turkey in Alabama. Ala. Game and Fish News 11(9):3-4.

Goodrum, P.D. 1940. A population study of the gray squirrel in eastern Texas. Texas Agr. Exp. Sta. Bull. 591. 34 pp.

Goodrum, P.D.,V.H. Reid, C.E. Boyd 1971. Acorn yields, characteristics, and management criteria of oaks for wildlife. Journal of Wildlife Management 35(3): 521-532.

Griffin, J.R. 1971. Oak regeneration in the upper Carmel Valley, California. Ecology 52(5):862-868.

Griffin, J.R. 1977. Oak woodlands. In Barbour, M.G. and J Major (eds.). Terrestrial vegetation of California. Wiley Interscience, NY. pp. 384-415.

Gumtow-Farrior, D.L. 1991. Cavity resources in Oregon white oak and Douglas-fir stands in the mid-Willamette Valley, Oregon. M.S. Thesis, Oregon State University, Corvallis, OR. 89 pp.

Gumtow-Farrior, D.L. and C.M. Gumtow-Farrior. 1992. Managing Oregon white oak communities for wildlife in Oregon's Willamette Valley: a problem analysis. Corvallis, OR: Oregon Department of Fish and Wildlife, Non-Game Program. 75 pp.

Habeck, J.R. 1961. The original vegetation of the mid-Willamette Valley, Oregon. Northwest Science 35(2):65-77.

Hagar, J.H. and M.A. Stern. 1997. Avifauna in oak woodland habitats of the Willamette Valley, Oregon 1994-1996. Unpublished report. U.S. Fish and Wildlife Migratory Birds-Nongame Program. 33 pp.

Halloran, A.F. 1943. Management of deer and cattle on Aransas National Wildlife Refuge, Texas. Journal of Wildlife Management 7(2):203-216.

Hannon, S.J., R.L. Mumme, W.D. Koenig, S. Spon, F.A. Pitelka. 1987. Poor acorn crop, dominance, and decline in numbers of acorn woodpeckers. Journal of Animal Ecology 56:197-207.

Hastings, M.S., S. Barnhart, and J.R. McBride. 1997. Restoration management of northern oak woodlands. In Pillsbury, N.H., J. Verner, W.D Tietje, tech. coords. Proceedings of a symposium on oak woodlands: ecology, management, and urban interface issues; 19-22 March 1996; San Luis Obispo, CA. Gen. Tech. Rep. PSW-GTR-160. Albany, CA; Pacific Southwest Research Station, USDA Forest Service. pp. 275-279.

Haynes, R.W., R.T. Graham, and T.M. Quigley, tech. eds. 1996. A framework for ecosystem management in the Interior Columbia Basin including portions of the Klamath and Great Basins. Gen. Tech Rep. PNW-GTR-374. Portland, OR; Pacific Northwest Research Station, USDA Forest Service. 66 pp.

Ingles, L.G. 1965. Mammals of the Pacific states. Stanford University Press, Stanford, CA. 506 pp.

Jensen M.E. and R. Everett. 1994. An overview of ecosystem management principles. In Jensen, M.E. and P.S. Bourgeron, tech eds. Volume II: Ecosystem management: principles and applications. Gen. Tech. Rep. PNW-GTR-318. Pacific Northwest Research Station, USDA, Forest Service. 376 pp.

Johannessen, C.L., W.A. Davenport, A. Millet, and S. McWilliams. 1971. The vegetation of the Willamette Valley. Association of American Geographers, Annals 61(2):286-302.

Keator, G. 1998. The life of an oak. Heyday Books and the California Oak Foundation. Berkeley and Oakland, California. 256 pp.

Kerns, S.J. 1980. Observations on wildlife abundance in several California black oak habitats in northern California. In Plumb, T.R., tech. coord. Proceedings of the symposium on the ecology, management, and utilization of California oaks, June 26-28, 1979; Claremont, CA. Gen. Tech Rep. PSW-44; Pacific Southwest Research Station, Forest Service, USDA.

Koenig, W.D. 1978. Ecological and evolutionary aspects of cooperative breeding in acorn wood-peckers of central coastal California. Ph.D. thesis, Univ. Calif. Berkeley.

Koenig, W.D. 1980. Acorn storage by acorn woodpeckers in an oak woodland: an energetics analysis. In Plumb, T.R., tech. coord. Proceedings of the symposium on the ecology, man-agement, and utilization of California oaks, June 26-28, 1979; Claremont, CA. Gen. Tech Rep. PSW-44; Pacific Southwest Research Station, USDA Forest Service.

Koenig, W.D. and R.L. Mumme. 1987. Population ecology of the cooperatively breeding acorn woodpecker. Monographs in population biology no. 24. Princeton Univ. Press; Princeton, New Jersey; 435 pp.

Lay, D.W. 1957. Some nutritional problems of deer in the southern pine type. Proc. Southeastern Assoc. Game and Fish Commissioners 10:53-58.

Lay, D.W. 1965. Fruit utilization of deer in southern pine forests. Journal of Wildlife Management 29(2):370-375.

Ligon, J.S. 1946. History and management of Merriam's wild turkey. New Mexico Game and Fish Comm. Bull. 84 pp.

Linduska, J.P. 1950. Ecology and land-use relationships of small mammals on a Michigan farm. Michigan Dept. Conserv., Game Div. 144 pp.

Longhurst, W.M., G.E. Connolly, B.M. Browning, and E.O. Garton. 1979. Food interrelationships of deer and sheep in parts of Mendocino and Lake Counties, California. Hilgardia.

Lorimar, C.G. 1993. Causes of the oak regeneration problem. In Loftis, D. and McGee, D.E., tech. eds. Oak regeneration: serious problems, practical recommendations. Symposium Proceedings; 1992 September 8-10; Knoxville, Tennessee. Presented by the Center for Oak Studies. Gen. Tech. Rep. SE-84. Asheville, NC; U.S. Department of Agriculture, Forest Service, Southeastern Forest Experiment Station. 319 pp.

MacRoberts, M.H. and B.R. MacRoberts. 1976. Social organization and behavior of the acorn woodpecker in central coastal California. Ornith. Monogr. 21:1-115.

Marshall, D.B., M. Chilcote, and H. Weeks. 1996. Species at risk: sensitive, threatened and endangered vertebrates of Oregon. 2nd edition. Oregon Department of Fish and Wildlife, Portland.

Martin, A.C., H.S. Zim, A.L. Nelson. 1951. American wildlife and plants: a guide to wildlife food habits. New York: Dover Publications, Inc. 500 pp.

Maser, C., J.M. Trappe, R.A. Nussbaum. 1978. Fungal-small mammal interrelationships with emphasis on Oregon coniferous forests. Ecology 59:799-809.

May, F.H., A.C. Martin, and T.E. Clarke. 1939. Early winter food preferences of the wild turkey on the George Washington National Forest,. Trans. 4th N. Am. Wildl. Conf.: 570-578.

McCulloch, W.F. 1940. Oregon oak – tree of conflict. American Forests 46(6):264-266, 286, 288.

McDonald, P. and M.W. Ritchie. 1994. Epicormic branching of California black oak: effect of stand and tree characteristics. Northwest Science 68(1): 6-10.

McGarigal, K. and W.C. McComb. 1992. Streamside versus upslope breeding bird communities in the central Oregon Coast Range. Journal of Wildlife Management 56:10-23.

Mellanby, K. 1968. The effects of some mammals and birds on regeneration of oak. J. Appl. Ecol. 5(4):359-366.

Menke, J.W. and M.E. Fry. 1980. Trends in oak utilization-fuelwood, mast production, animal use. In Plumb, T.R., tech. coord. Proceedings of the symposium on the ecology, management, and utilization of California oaks, June 26-28, 1979; Claremont, CA. Gen. Tech Rep. PSW-44; Pacific Southwest Research Station, USDA Forest Service.

Morrison, P.H. and F.J. Swanson. 1990. Fire history and pattern in a Cascade Range landscape. Gen. Tech. Rep. PNW-GTR-254. Portland, OR: Pacific Northwest Research Station, USDA, Forest Service. 77 pp.

Mosby, H.S. and C.O. Handley 1943. The wild turkey in Virginia, its status, life history and management. Va. Comm. of Game and Inland Fisheries, Richmond. 288 pp.

Nichol, A.A. 1938. Experimental feeding of deer. Univ. of Arizona. Agr. Exp. Sta. Tech. Bull. 75. 39 pp.

Oregon Climate Service 1998. Climate data home page. World Wide Web Page, _ HYPERLINK http://www.ocs.orst.edu/ocs_data.html _ www.ocs.orst.edu/ocs_data.html_. [Accessed October 1, 1998].

Pacific Wildlife Research. 1998. Survey of Willamette Valley oak woodlands herpetofauna 1997-1998. Unpublished report for the Oregon Department of Fish and Wildlife, Northwest Region.

Parks, C.G., E.L. Bull, and T.R. Torgersen. 1997. Field guide for the identification of snags and logs in the Interior Columbia River Basin. Gen. Tech. Rep. PNW-GTR-390. Portland OR: Pacific Northwest Research Station, USDA Forest Service. 40 pp.

Pavlik, B.M., Muick, P.C., Johnson, S. and M. Popper. 1991. Oaks of California. Cachuma Press and California Oak Foundation. Los Olivos, California. 184 pp.

Pearson, A.M. 1943. White-tails like acorns. Alabama Conservation 15(6):8-9.

Pearson, A.M. and C.R. Burnett. 1940. Deer food in Black Warrior National Forest, Alabama Game and Fish News, 11(8):3-4.

Piekielek, W. and T.S. Burton. 1975. A black bear population study in northern California. Calif. Fish and Game 61(1):4-25.

Pillsbury, N.H., J. Verner and W.D. Tietje, tech coords. 1997. Proceedings of a symposium on oak woodlands: ecology, management, and urban interface issues; 19-22 March 1996; San Luis Obispo, CA. Gen. Tech. Rep. PSW-GTR-160. Albany CA; Pacific Southwest Research Station, Forest Service, U.S. Department of Agriculture.

Reed, L.J. and N.G. Sugihara. 1987. Northern oak woodlands—ecosystem in jeopardy or is it already too late. In Plumb, T.R., and N.H. Pillsbury, tech. coordinators. Proceedings of the symposium on multiple-use management of California's hardwood resources, November 12-14, 1986; San Luis Obispo, CA. Gen. Tech. Rep. PSW-100; Pacific Southwest Research Station, Forest Service, USDA.

Ryan L.A. and A.B. Carey. 1995a. Biology and management of the western gray squirrel and Oregon white oak woodlands: with emphasis on Puget Trough. Gen. Tech. Rep. PNW-GTR-348. Portland, OR: U.S. Department of Agriculture, Forest Service, Pacific Northwest Research Station. 36 p.

Ryan L.A. and A.B. Carey. 1995b. Distribution and habitat of the western gray squirrel (*Sciurus griseus*) on Ft. Lewis, Washington. Northwest Science 69(3):204-216.

Sanders, E. 1941. A preliminary report on the study of the white-tailed deer in the Edwards Plateau, Texas. Journal of Wildlife Management 5(2):182-190.

Sharp, W.M. and V.G. Sprague. 1967. Flowering and fruiting in the white oaks: pistillate flowering, acorn development, weather, and yields. Ecology 48(2):243-251.

Sisk, T.D., N.M. Hadad, P.R. Ehrlich. 1997. Bird assemblages in patchy woodlands: modeling the effects of edge and matrix habitats. Ecological Applications. 7(4): 1170-1180.

Smith, W.A. and B. Browning. 1967. Wild turkey food habits in San Luis Obispo County, California. Calif. Fish and Game, 53(4):246-253.

Sprague F.L. and H.P. Hansen.1946. Forest succession in the McDonald Forest, Willamette Valley, Oregon. Northwest Science. 20:89-98.

Stein, W.I. 1990. *Quercus garryana* Dougl. Ex Hook. Oregon white oak. In Silvics of North America Vol. 2, hardwoods. USDA, Forest Service, Pacific Northwest Forest and Range Experiment Station. Handbook 654. pp. 650-660.

Stienecker, W.E. and B.M. Browning. 1970. Food habits of the western gray squirrel. California Department of Fish and Game. 56:36-48.

Sugihara, N.G. and L.J. Reed. 1987a. Prescribed fire for restoration and maintenance of bald hills oak woodlands. In Plumb, T.R. and N.H. Pillsbury, tech. coords. Proceedings of the symposium on multiple-use management of California's hardwood resources, November 12-14, 1986; San Luis Obispo, CA. Gen. Tech. Rep. PSW-100; Pacific Southwest Research Station, USDA Forest Service.

Sugihara, N.G. and L.J. Reed. 1987b. Vegetation ecology of the bald hills oak woodlands of Redwood National Park. Redwood National Park technical report 21. National Park Service, Redwood National Park. Orick, California. 78 pp.

Swanson, F.J., J.A. Jones, and G.E. Grant. 1997. The physical environment as a basis for managing ecosystems. In K.A. Kohm and J.F. Franklin, eds. Creating a forestry for the 21st century: the science of ecosystem management. Island Press, Washington, DC. 475 pp.

Tappeiner J. and P. McDonald. 1980. Preliminary recommendations for managing California black oak in the Sierra Nevada. In Plumb, T.R., tech. coord. Proceedings of the symposium on the ecology, management, and utilization of California oaks, June 26-28, 1979; Claremont, CA. Gen. Tech Rep. PSW-44; Pacific Southwest Research Station, USDA Forest Service.

Taylor, W.P. 1944. Live oak acorns and fruits of the black persimmon in the November diet of the white-tailed deer in Mason County, Texas. 882 Congress Progress Report, Texas Agr. Exp. Sta., A & M College, Texas.

Thilenius, J.F. 1964. Synecology of the white-oak (*Quercus garryana* Douglas) woodlands of the Willamette Valley, Oregon., Oregon State University, Corvallis. Ph.D. Thesis. 151 pp.

Thilenius, J.F. 1968. The Quercus garryana forests of the Willamette Valley, Oregon. Ecology 49(6):1124-1133.

Thomas, J.W. 1996. Forest service perspective on ecosystem management. Ecological Applications. 6(3):703-705.

Towle, J.C. 1982. Changing geography of Willamette Valley woodlands. Oregon Historical Quarterly. 83(1):66-87.

Uhlig, H.G. 1956. The gray squirrel in West Virginia. West Virginia Conserv. Comm. Bull. 3. 83 pp.

Uhlig, H.G. and R.W. Bailey. 1952. Wild turkey in West Virginia. Journal of Wildlife Management 16(1):24-32.

U.S. Department of the Interior, Bureau of Land Management. 1995. Fish and Wildlife 2000 program strategy. USDI BLM, Eugene District, Oregon. 47 pp.

Van Dersal, W.R. 1940. Utilization of oaks by birds and mammals. Journal of Wildlife Management 4(4):404-428.

Verner, J. 1980. Birds of California oak habitats – management implications. In Plumb, T.R., tech. coord. Proceedings of the symposium on the ecology, management, and utilization of California oaks, June 26-28, 1979; Claremont, CA. Gen. Tech Rep. PSW-44; Pacific Southwest Research Station, Forest Service, USDA.

Verner, J. 1983. Significance of oak woodlands in maintaining the richness of California's avifauna . In Brown, S. and P.A. Bowler, eds. Proceedings of the California oak heritage conservation conference, 1983 March 11-12. Irvine, CA.

Wilson, R.A., P. Manley, B.R. Noon. 1991. Covariance patterns among birds and vegetation in a California oak woodland. Standiford, R.B. (tech. coord.) USDA For. Gen. Tech. Rep. PSW-126.

APPENDIX A

List of Wildlife Species
Found in the

Species	Dry hillside/ grass forb	Deciduois- hardwood	Conifer- hardwood forest	Shrub-forest edge	Brown Grass-forest edge
			Habitats		
clouded salamander			1	2	1
ensatina		1	1	1	
western redback salamander		2	2		
northern alligator lizard		1	1	2	2
southern alligator lizard		1	1	2	2
western fence lizard	1	2	1		2
western skink		1	1		1
rubber boa			1		1
racer	1	1	1		1
sharptail snake	1	1	1		2
ringneck snake		2	1		1
gopher snake	1	1	2		
western terrestrial garter snake	2	1	1		2

[1] Habitats: Information is for breeding use only. 1=primary habitat; 2=secondary habitat. Habitat was scored as primary if any of six stand conditions were listed as primary breeding habitat. If species only used old-growth, no score was given.

Potentially Occurring in the Habitats
Surveyed Sites

| 1985[1] | | | | | | Csuti et al. 1995[2] | Hagar and Stern 1977[3] |
| | Snags | | | Cavities | | | |
Grass-forb hills	Deciduous-hardwoods	Coniferous hardwoods	Suggested dbh (inches)	Minimum tree height (feet)		Oak	Top 50 birds
		x					
						x	
						x/pine	

[2] Species use of oak habitat
[3] The 50 most frequent bird species observed in 9 oak woodland sites in the Willamette Valley, Oregon, 1994-1996. Numbers refer to ranking in abundance (1-50).

| Species | Habitats | | | | Brown |
	Dry hillside/ grass forb	Deciduois- hardwood	Conifer- hardwood forest	Shrub-forest edge	Grass-forest edge
northwestern garter snake	2	2	2	2	1
common garter snake		1	1		
western rattlesnake	1	2	2		
turkey vulture	2	2	2		
black-shouldered kite		2			1
sharp-shinned hawk			1		
Cooper's hawk		1	1		
northern goshawk			2		
red-tailed hawk		1	1	2	2
American kestrel		1	2	1	1
ring-neck pheasant	2	2	2		2
blue grouse		2	2	1	1
ruffed grouse		1	1	1	1
wild turkey		1		2	2
California quail	1	1		2	
mountain quail	2	1	2	2	2

[1] Habitats: Information is for breeding use only. 1=primary habitat; 2=secondary habitat. Habitat was scored as primary if any of six stand conditions were listed as primary breeding habitat. If species only used old-growth, no score was given.

| 1985[1] | | | | | Csuti et al. 1995[2] | Hagar and Stern 1977[3] |
| Snags | | | Cavities | | | |
Grass-forb hills	Deciduous-hardwoods	Coniferous hardwoods	Suggested dbh (inches)	Minimum tree height (feet)	Oak	Top 50 birds
x	x	x				
		x			x	
	x	x			x	
x	x	x				
	x	x				45
x	x		17	20		
						48
					x	
					x	

[2] Species use of oak habitat
[3] The 50 most frequent bird species observed in 9 oak woodland sites in the Willamette Valley, Oregon, 1994-1996. Numbers refer to ranking in abundance (1-50).

Species	Dry hillside/ grass forb	Deciduois- hardwood	Conifer- hardwood forest	Shrub-forest edge	Grass-forest edge	Brown
			Habitats			
band-tailed pigeon		1	1	1	1	
mourning dove		1	1	2	1	
common barn owl		2	2	1	1	
western screech owl		1	2	1	1	
great horn owl		1	1	1	1	
northern pygmy owl		2	1	1	1	
barred owl		2	1			
northern saw-whet owl		2	2	1	1	
common nighthawk	1	1	1	1	1	
common poorwill	1	1		2	2	
Vaux's swift		2	2	1	1	
Anna's hummingbird		1		1	2	
rufous hummingbird		1	1	1	1	
acorn woodpecker		1	2	2	1	
red-breasted sapsucker		2	2	2	2	
northern flicker		1	1	2	1	

[1] Habitats: Information is for breeding use only. 1=primary habitat; 2=secondary habitat. Habitat was scored as primary if any of six stand conditions were listed as primary breeding habitat. If species only used old-growth, no score was given.

| 1985[1] | | | | | Csuti et al. 1995[2] | Hagar and Stern 1977[3] |
| | Snags | | Cavities | | | |
Grass-forb hills	Deciduous-hardwoods	Coniferous hardwoods	Suggested dbh (inches)	Minimum tree height (feet)	Oak	Top 50 birds
					x	46
					x	37
	x	x	25	20	x	
	x	x	17	20	x	
x	x	x	25	30		
	x	x	17	30		
		x	25	30		
	x	x	17	20		
					x	
	x	x	25	40		
						38
	x	x	17	30	x	50
	x	x	15	20		33
	x	x	17	10		34

[2] Species use of oak habitat
[3] The 50 most frequent bird species observed in 9 oak woodland sites in the Willamette Valley, Oregon, 1994-1996. Numbers refer to ranking in abundance (1-50).

Species	Dry hillside/ grass forb	Deciduois-hardwood	Conifer-hardwood forest	Shrub-forest edge	Grass-forest edge
					Brown
			Habitats		
downy woodpecker		1	2		
hairy woodpecker			2		
olive-sided flycatcher			1	2	2
western wood pewee		1	1		1
willow flycatcher		2			1
Hammond's flycatcher			2	1	1
western kingbird		2		2	1
horned lark	1				
purple martin		2	2	1	1
tree swallow		2	2		
violet-green swallow		1	2		
Stellar's jay		2	1	2	2
scrub jay		1	2	1	2
American crow		1	2	2	2
common raven		1	1	2	2
black-capped chickadee		1	1	1	

[1] Habitats: Information is for breeding use only. 1=primary habitat; 2=secondary habitat. Habitat was scored as primary if any of six stand conditions were listed as primary breeding habitat. If species only used old-growth, no score was given.

| 1985[1] | | | | | Csuti et al. 1995[2] | Hagar and Stern 1977[3] |
| | Snags | | Cavities | | | |
Grass-forb hills	Deciduous-hardwoods	Coniferous hardwoods	Suggested dbh (inches)	Minimum tree height (feet	Oak	Top 50 birds
	x	x	11	10		28
		x	15	20		41
	x	x				
					x	2
						49
	x				x	
			15	10		
	x	x	15	20		36
	x	x	15	20		
						31
					x	23
						44
	x	x	9	10		4

[2] Species use of oak habitat
[3] The 50 most frequent bird species observed in 9 oak woodland sites in the Willamette Valley, Oregon, 1994-1996. Numbers refer to ranking in abundance (1-50).

	Habitats[1]				Brown
Species	Dry hillside/grass forb	Deciduois-hardwood	Conifer-hardwood forest	Shrub-forest edge	Grass-forest edge
chestnut-backed chickadee		2	1		
bushtit		1	2	1	
red-breasted nuthatch			1		
white-breasted nuthatch		1	1		
brown creeper		2	1		
Bewick's wren		1	2	1	
house wren		1		1	
winter wren			1	1	
golden-crowned kinglet			2		
western bluebird		1	1	1	1
Townsend's solitaire			1	1	2
Swainson's thrush		2	2	1	2
hermit thrush			1	1	2
American robin		1	1	1	1
varied thrush			1	1	2
wrentit		1		1	

[1] Habitats: Information is for breeding use only. 1=primary habitat; 2=secondary habitat. Habitat was scored as primary if any of six stand conditions were listed as primary breeding habitat. If species only used old-growth, no score was given.

| 1985[1] | | | | | Csuti et al. 1995[2] | Hagar and Stern 1977[3] |
| Snags | | | Cavities | | | |
Grass-forb hills	Deciduous-hardwoods	Coniferous hardwoods	Suggested dbh (inches)	Minimum tree height (feet)	Oak	Top 50 birds
	x	x	9	10		43
						39
	x	x	17	20		24
	x	x	17	20	x	17
	x	x	15	20		13
	x					15
	x		15	10	x	6
		x				30
	x		15	10	x	
						7
					x	5
					x	

[2] Species use of oak habitat
[3] The 50 most frequent bird species observed in 9 oak woodland sites in the Willamette Valley, Oregon, 1994-1996. Numbers refer to ranking in abundance (1-50).

Species	Dry hillside/ grass forb	Deciduois- hardwood	Conifer- hardwood forest	Shrub-forest edge	Grass-forest edge
					Brown
			Habitats		
cedar waxwing		2	2		
European starling		1	2	1	1
solitary vireo		1	1		
Hutton's vireo		1	2	1	
warbling vireo		1	2	1	
orange-crowned warbler		1	1	1	
Nashville warbler		1	1	1	
yellow-rumped warbler			1	1	2
black-throated gray warbler		1	1	1	
MacGillivray's warbler			2	1	
Wilson's warbler			1	1	
yellow-breasted chat		2		2	
western tananger		2	1	1	2
black-headed grosbeak		1	1	1	1
lazuli bunting		1	2		
rufous-sided towhee		1	1	1	

[1] Habitats: Information is for breeding use only. 1=primary habitat; 2=secondary habitat. Habitat was scored as primary if any of six stand conditions were listed as primary breeding habitat. If species only used old-growth, no score was given.

| 1985[1] | | | | | | Csuti et al. 1995[2] | Hagar and Stern 1977[3] |
| | Snags | | | Cavities | | | |
Grass-forb hills	Deciduous-hardwoods	Coniferous hardwoods	Suggested dbh (inches)	Minimum tree height (feet	Oak	Top 50 birds
						19
			15	10		12
						20
					x	35
					x	42
					x	3
					x	
						40
						27
					x (?)	16
					x	
					x	29

[2] Species use of oak habitat
[3] The 50 most frequent bird species observed in 9 oak woodland sites in the Willamette Valley, Oregon, 1994-1996. Numbers refer to ranking in abundance (1-50).

Species	Dry hillside/ grass forb	Deciduois-hardwood	Conifer-hardwood forest	Shrub-forest edge	Grass-forest edge
brown towhee		1			
chipping sparrow		1	1	1	1
vesper sparrow	1	1			
lark sparrow	1	1		2	
savannah sparrow	2	2			
fox sparrow		1	1	1	2
song sparrow		1	1	2	2
white-crowned sparrow	1	2	2	2	
dark-eyed junco		2	1	1	1
western meadowlark	1	2			
Brewer's blackbird		1	1	1	
brown-headed cowbird		1	1	1	1
northern oriole		1		1	1
purple finch		1	1	1	1
house finch		1	2	1	1
pine siskin		2	2	1	1

[1] Habitats: Information is for breeding use only. 1=primary habitat; 2=secondary habitat. Habitat was scored as primary if any of six stand conditions were listed as primary breeding habitat. If species only used old-growth, no score was given.

| 1985[1] | Snags | | | Cavities | | Csuti et al. 1995[2] | Hagar and Stern 1977[3] |
	Grass-forb hills	Deciduous-hardwoods	Coniferous hardwoods	Suggested dbh (inches)	Minimum tree height (feet)	Oak	Top 50 birds
							21
							25
							8
							11
						x	26
							10
		x	x	15	10		

[2] Species use of oak habitat
[3] The 50 most frequent bird species observed in 9 oak woodland sites in the Willamette Valley, Oregon, 1994-1996. Numbers refer to ranking in abundance (1-50).

Species	Dry hillside/ grass forb	Deciduois-hardwood	Conifer-hardwood forest	Shrub-forest edge	Grass-forest edge
					Brown
			Habitats		
lesser goldfinch		1	2	1	
American goldfinch		1	2	1	
evening grosbeak			2		
Virginia opossum		1	2		
vagrant shrew		2	2	1	1
Trowbridge's shrew			2		
shrew-mole			1		
coast mole			1	2	2
Townsend's mole			2	2	1
big brown bat		2	2		
silver-haired bat			2		
hoary bat			2		
California myotis			2		
long-eared myotis			2		
little brown myotis		2	2		
fringed myotis		2	2		

[1] Habitats: Information is for breeding use only. 1=primary habitat; 2=secondary habitat. Habitat was scored as primary if any of six stand conditions were listed as primary breeding habitat. If species only used old-growth, no score was given.

| 1985[1] | | | | | Csuti et al. 1995[2] | Hagar and Stern 1977[3] |
| Snags | | | Cavities | | | |
Grass-forb hills	Deciduous-hardwoods	Coniferous hardwoods	Suggested dbh (inches)	Minimum tree height (feet)	Oak	Top 50 birds
					x	
						14
						47
	x	x	25	10		
	x	x	17	20		
	x	x	17	20		
		x	17	10		
	x	x	17	10		
	x	x	17	10		
	x	x	17	10		

[2] Species use of oak habitat
[3] The 50 most frequent bird species observed in 9 oak woodland sites in the Willamette Valley, Oregon, 1994-1996. Numbers refer to ranking in abundance (1-50).

Species	Dry hillside/ grass forb	Deciduois-hardwood	Conifer-hardwood forest	Shrub-forest edge	Grass-forest edge
					Brown
			Habitats		
long-legged myotis		1	1		
Yuma myotis		2	1		
pallid bat					
coyote	1	1	1	2	1
gray fox		1	1		
red fox	1	1	1	1	
black bear		2	2		
raccoon	2	1	1		
striped skunk		1	2	2	2
long-tailed weasel	1	2	2	2	2
ermine		2	1		
mink	2	2	2		
spotted skunk		1	1	2	2
mountain lion		2	2		
bobcat		2	2	2	2
elk		1	1	1	1

[1] Habitats: Information is for breeding use only. 1=primary habitat; 2=secondary habitat. Habitat was scored as primary if any of six stand conditions were listed as primary breeding habitat. If species only used old-growth, no score was given.

| 1985[1] | | | | | | Csuti et al. 1995[2] | Hagar and Stern 1977[3] |
| Grass-forb hills | Snags | | Cavities | | | Oak | Top 50 birds |
	Deciduous-hardwoods	Coniferous hardwoods	Suggested dbh (inches)	Minimum tree height (feet)			
	x	x	17	10		x	
	x	x	17	10		x	
	x		17	20		x	
	x	x	29	10		x	
			29	10			
x	x	x	25	10			
x	x	x	17	10			
	x	x	15	10			
	x	x	25	10			
	x	x	29	10			

[2] Species use of oak habitat
[3] The 50 most frequent bird species observed in 9 oak woodland sites in the Willamette Valley, Oregon, 1994-1996. Numbers refer to ranking in abundance (1-50).

ASSESSMENT OF OAK WOODLAND RESOURCES IN BLM'S EUGENE DISTRICT

Species	Dry hillside/ grass forb	Deciduois-hardwood	Conifer-hardwood forest	Shrub-forest edge	Grass-forest edge
					Brown
		Habitats			
mule deer		1	1	1	1
mountain beaver			2	1	1
western gray squirrel		1	1	1	2
California ground squirrel	1	2	2		2
Townsend's chipmunk		1	2	2	2
Douglas' squirrel			2	2	2
Botta's pocket gopher	1				
Camas pocket gopher		1	2	2	1
western pocket gopher		1	2	2	1
bushy-tailed woodrat		2	2	2	
dusky-footed woodrat		1	1	2	
deer mouse	2	1	1	1	2
western harvest mouse	1				
white-footed vole		2			
California vole	1	1			
gray-tailed vole		2			2

[1] Habitats: Information is for breeding use only. 1=primary habitat; 2=secondary habitat. Habitat was scored as primary if any of six stand conditions were listed as primary breeding habitat. If species only used old-growth, no score was given.

| 1985[1] | | | | | | Csuti et al. 1995[2] | Hagar and Stern 1977[3] |
| | Snags | | | Cavities | | | |
Grass-forb hills	Deciduous-hardwoods	Coniferous hardwoods	Suggested dbh (inches)	Minimum tree height (feet	Oak	Top 50 birds
	x	x	17	20	x	
					x	
		x	17	20		
	x	x	17	10		
x	x	x	15	10		

[2] Species use of oak habitat
[3] The 50 most frequent bird species observed in 9 oak woodland sites in the Willamette Valley, Oregon, 1994-1996. Numbers refer to ranking in abundance (1-50).

Species	Habitats				Brown
	Dry hillside/ grass forb	Deciduois-hardwood	Conifer-hardwood forest	Shrub-forest edge	Grass-forest edge
long-tailed vole		2		2	2
creeping vole		1	1		1
Townsend's vole		2	2		2
Pacific jumping mouse		1	1		
porcupine			1		
black-tailed jack rabbit	1	1			2
European rabbit			2	2	2
brush rabbit		1	1	2	2
eastern cottontail		1		2	2

[1] Habitats: Information is for breeding use only. 1=primary habitat; 2=secondary habitat. Habitat was scored as primary if any of six stand conditions were listed as primary breeding habitat. If species only used old-growth, no score was given.

1985[1]						Csuti et al. 1995[2]	Hagar and Stern 1977[3]
	Snags			Cavities			
Grass-forb hills	Deciduous-hardwoods	Coniferous hardwoods	Suggested dbh (inches)	Minimum tree height (feet	Oak	Top 50 birds

[2] Species use of oak habitat
[3] The 50 most frequent bird species observed in 9 oak woodland sites in the Willamette Valley, Oregon, 1994-1996. Numbers refer to ranking in abundance (1-50).

1. AGENCY USE ONLY (Leave blank)	2. REPORT DATE June 2000	3. REPORT TYPE AND DATES COVERED Final

4. TITLE AND SUBTITLE Assessment of Oak Woodland Resources in BLM's Eugene District Lane County, Oregon Technical Note 406	5. FUNDING NUMBERS
6. AUTHOR(S) David G. Chiller, David G. Vesely, and William I. Dean	

7. PERFORMING ORGANIZATION NAME(S) AND ADDRESS(ES) U.S. Department of the Interior Bureau of Land Management National Applied Resource Sciences Center P.O. Box 25047 Denver, CO 80225-0047	8. PERFORMING ORGANIZATION REPORT NUMBER BLM/OR/WA/PL-00/052+6635

9. SPONSORING/MONITORING AGENCY NAME(S) AND ADDRESS(ES)	10. SPONSORING/MONITORING AGENCY REPORT NUMBER

11. SUPPLEMENTARY NOTES

12a. DISTRIBUTION/AVAILABILITY STATEMENT	12b. DISTRIBUTION CODE

13. ABSTRACT (Maximum 200 words)

Because of the significant loss of oak (*Quercus* spp.) habitat and the subsequent increased value placed on oak woodlands for wildlife habitat, the preservation and restoration of native oak woodlands has become a priority for land managers and conservationists in the Western United States. In 1998, reconnaissance surveys were conducted on 13 oak woodland sites managed by the Bureau of Land Management's (BLM's) Eugene District in Lane County, Oregon. The sites were classified as either meadow-type communities or woodland-type communities; oak patches within the sites were delineated; and the topographic features, vegetation structure, and composition of the sites were characterized. Current conditions were then compared with conditions documented in historical records. In addition, the wildlife species most likely occurring on the sites were identified. Literature from oak woodland studies was then reviewed to determine whether certain management and restoration methods, such as eliminating conifer encroachment and thinning closed canopy stands, would be effective in addressing conditions observed at the BLM sites.

14. SUBJECT TERMS Oak woodlands Wildlife habitat Vegetation	15. NUMBER OF PAGES 98 including covers
	16. PRICE CODE

17. SECURITY CLASSIFICATION OF REPORT Unclassified	18. SECURITY CLASSIFICATION OF THIS PAGE Unclassified	19. SECURITY CLASSIFICATION OF ABSTRACT Unclassified	20. LIMITATION OF ABSTRACT UL